T0330534

ROUTLEDGE LIBRARY EDITIONS:
THE OIL INDUSTRY

Volume 2

CHRONOLOGY
OF VENEZUELAN OIL

CHRONOLOGY
OF VENEZUELAN OIL

ANIBAL R. MARTINEZ

LONDON AND NEW YORK

First published in 1969 by George Allen & Unwin Ltd

This edition first published in 2024
by Routledge
4 Park Square, Milton Park, Abingdon, Oxon OX14 4RN

and by Routledge
605 Third Avenue, New York, NY 10158

Routledge is an imprint of the Taylor & Francis Group, an informa business

British Library Cataloguing in Publication Data
A catalogue record for this book is available from the British Library

ISBN: 978-1-032-55944-5 (Set)
ISBN: 978-1-032-56874-4 (Volume 2) (hbk)
ISBN: 978-1-032-56876-8 (Volume 2) (pbk)
ISBN: 978-1-003-43747-5 (Volume 2) (ebk)

DOI: 10.4324/9781003437475

Publisher's Note
The publisher has gone to great lengths to ensure the quality of this reprint but
points out that some imperfections in the original copies may be apparent.

Disclaimer
The publisher has made every effort to trace copyright holders and would
welcome correspondence from those they have been unable to trace.

CHRONOLOGY
OF
VENEZUELAN
OIL

by

ANIBAL R. MARTINEZ

London

GEORGE ALLEN AND UNWIN LTD

RUSKIN HOUSE   MUSEUM STREET

PRINTED IN GREAT BRITAIN
in 12 pt Bembo type
BY PURNELL AND SONS LTD
PAULTON (SOMERSET) AND LONDON

PREFACE

During the period I was doing graduate work at Stanford University, from 1952 to 1954, I used to spend a considerable amount of time at the Branner Library doing research on various subjects of petroleum engineering and geology, and preparing many reports. Whenever possible I chose subjects relating to the petroleum industry of my own country, Venezuela, and somehow acquired the habit of jotting down notes of interesting events which had occurred during the development of the Venezuelan oil industry, so much so in fact, that I succeeded in earning two credit units for a rough, preliminary compilation of 289 events, which I entitled *"Chronology—Venezuelan Oil"*.

I never lost the habit of note-taking and over the course of the years have registered on any scrap of paper available, further important events which I came upon during the course of my studies, the perusal of scientific publications, magazines and other documents, and also in the books I consulted. Everywhere I went I took along the two small wooden boxes I had originally bought at the Stanford Bookstore and in which I kept my collection of cards on to which I had transcribed by hand the data accumulated at anonymous times.

When Creole Petroleum Corporation sent me to work on loan for the old Jersey Production Research Company at Tulsa in 1957, I had the opportunity to put some kind of order into the job I had started during my time at Stanford and of actualizing my record card collection for the last six years. At Tulsa I found invaluable new sources and material at my disposal in the very compact and good petroleum library of the JPR Co. This seems as good a time as any to inform the reader that I have in all instances purposely confined my sources to books, scientific magazines, professional periodicals, proceedings, memoirs, etc. May I mention that no confidential, restricted, or otherwise classified material, not intended for the public, was used for the compilation of this chronology; any persons interested could have had access to the sources I consulted.

5

The final impulse towards the completion of this record of annals of the Venezuelan petroleum industry took place while working for the Organization of the Petroleum Exporting Countries (OPEC). I used the facilities of the small, but very good library of the Information Centre, built up since OPEC's establishment in 1960. To cover the earliest records of historical value in the industry during the period from the sixteenth to the nineteenth century, I used the collections contained in Vienna's magnificent Oesterreichische Nationalbibliothek, and, with respect to the literature of the early scientific papers, say, since 1840 and in particular the second half of last century and first two decades of the present, I used the very complete library of the Austrian Geologisches Bundesanstalt.

It should not be cause for disconcert that I cannot recall the exact date when I commenced work on my chronology of events of the development of the Venezuelan petroleum industry—it was merely the one event I did not record.

I would like to mention that the research for this work has been carried out in the free time at my disposal, while working for Jersey or at OPEC, and has in no way interfered with my normal duties; neither of them, or any other public, or private enterprise, has directed or influenced my work. Therefore, mistakes, misrepresentations, or omissions are my sole responsibility.

This book is dedicated to you, Mary, sweet companion of my post-graduate years at Stanford, of my early career with Creole and JPRCo, and of the period of my appointment to OPEC. In Palo Alto, Tulsa and Vienna; as well as the time in between in Maracaibo and Geneva—and always.

6

CONTENTS

INTRODUCTION

As I have not tried to make observations on the motives, causes and consequences of the events recorded, this book is not in the true sense of the word a history. I have merely attempted to ascertain the exact dates of past events and to arrange them in their proper chronological order.

Chronologies are useful for scholars, teachers, executives, professionalists and technicians, as well as students and those who have continual need for quick reference to dates of occurrences. Therefore, this fact makes it a *sine qua non* condition that a chronology should be incontestable for accuracy. My efforts have been directed to achieve this end. I have painstakingly checked and cross-checked my sources in order to arrive at a satisfactory result. Whenever possible, I have given the day and month of the occurrence in question. Unfortunately, in some instances I have been unable to obtain the exact reference and have, therefore, merely listed the event at the commencement of the respective year. In other cases, the nature of the event recorded permitted me only an approximation to the month, and is listed likewise— at the beginning of each month.

I have endeavoured to cover all aspects of the Venezuelan petroleum industry's historical evolution: technical, legal, economic, social and political.

There were rare instances when what might be taken as discrepancies arose. The difficulty was not, in this case, due to the reliability of the source of information, but rather to existing physical conditions, or to the possibility of slight variations in the interpretation of definitions.

Due to geological circumstances, occurrence of oilfields varies tremendously from one sedimentary basin to the next. An oilfield is the specific area of the earth which is vertically underlain by hydrocarbon reservoirs, which in turn are defined as the geological features where petroleum or natural gas have accumulated. In the overwhelming majority of cases, a field is made up of more than one reservoir at varying depths under the earth's surface.

There are six sedimentary basins in Venezuela, namely the Maracaibo, Gulf of Venezuela, Falcón, Barinas, Cariaco and Maturín basins. By far the most important petroliferous regions are in the Maracaibo basin; the fields are generally few in number but rather large. The discrepancies to which I refer stem in this case from the extensiveness of some of the fields. In the Bolívar Coastal field, for instance, operational units were discovered over a period of decades, far apart. The first completion in the field was made without those involved realizing the true value and meaning of the deposits they had tapped. In this chronology then, I have recorded the completion dates of the first wells in the most important areas inland and offshore in the "BCF"—as it is usually referred to in oil industry jargon. I have to add that I consider it quite incorrect to state, for example, that "the Lagunillas field" is the one which has so far had the largest volume of production in Venezuela, because such a "field" is merely a surface bounded by absolutely arbitrary and meaningless lines.

The Maturín basin oilfields, by contrast, are generally small but large in number; an almost insoluble problem is posed by the identification of each true natural unit, especially on account of the existing and most confusing nomenclature developed by various operators in the area and superimposed on the complex geological picture. The question therefore might be not whether a particular date is that of the discovery of such-and-such a field, but whether the field exists at all. As the reader will agree, any blame in these instances should not be put on the chronology.

It should be mentioned that there is no refuge in the publications of the Venezuelan Ministry of Mines and Hydrocarbons. Not only problems of nomenclature or difficulties of limitation of areas remain unsolved, but the picture is made even more confused due to the fact that the Ministry has its own method of reporting production and other information on the basis of, again, very arbitrary limits, areas developed over the years by the local field inspectors of the Technical Office of Hydrocarbons.

Another reason for possible discrepancies can be connected to what exactly is the discovery date of a field. I would define this as the moment when a successful test is completed in an exploratory well in a hitherto undeveloped area. This gives proof of the existence of commercial quantities of hydrocarbons in the prospect surveyed. In practice, however, successful discovery tests are seldom reported, so that in the oil industry literature one can only find the date of final completion of a well; which means that a multitude of technical, or non-technical factors might have prolonged—at times by months, or years—the period elapsing between the first test and the final disposal of the well. The completion date of the first commercial well is given in this book as that of the discovery of the field. Nevertheless, unanimity might not always be possible: although most reliable literature sources report the discovery date of the Mene Grande oilfield—the first one of importance found in Venezuela—to have occurred on April 15, 1914, some references show April 18, 1914. And then, the golden anniversary celebration of the field's discovery, claimed to be the starting point of the country's oil industry, took place on July 31, 1964.

A chronology somehow causes a flattening effect on the events reported, perhaps because the information is reduced to a list somewhat insipid and uniform. Certainly, the Hydrocarbons Law of March 13, 1943 is much more significant for the history of Venezuelan oil than that of July 18, 1928, or the discovery of flush Cretaceous production in the deeper reservoirs of the La Paz field is an event many times more important than the discovery of the small Quiroz field—something which for me, however, is of great personal value as it was here that I had my first professional assignment in subsurface geology to "scout" for Creole the drilling, progress and results of Shell's QZ-1.

Concerning oil- and gasfields, I give the name of the discovery well and the operator, as well as the location. I have then further indicated the relative importance of the field, by calling it "small", "one-well field", or a similar expression, when the find is indeed small in size. At the other end of the scale, I have clearly labelled the "giant" fields.

After decades of oil industry development, a limited number of fields in Venezuela have resources large enough to entitle them to the classification of "giant". These are, by definition, fields with an ultimate production volume estimated at 100 million barrels or more. Usually it takes a number of years before a new discovery reaches the "giant" category. Up to the end of 1966, a total of forty-four giant oilfields had been recognized in Venezuela. The Bolívar Coastal field, of course, is enormous and it contains at least two dozen "giant reservoirs". The BCF is perhaps the accumulation with the largest resources in the world, 16,500 million barrels. Some, who in their maps perhaps show the Urdaneta field as a number of isolated hexagons or circles of arbitrary size surrounding wildcats successfully completed during the last decade along the western shores of Lake Maracaibo, or who profess an intimate knowledge of the geological problems and the rash operational nomenclature of the Maturín basin, might disagree with me on labelling this or that field "giant". But this still does not change the accuracy of the chronology.

Antecedents of Venezuelan oil legislation are found in the *Fuero Viejo de Castilla,* the *Royal Ordinances on mining for the Colonies in the New World,* the *Quito decree of Simón Bolívar.* First laws were on mining, and then later on especially for hydro-carbons. Petroleum laws are equally important to both Venezuela and Venezuelans as legislation on income tax, because the amount of fiscal revenues deriving from the exploitation of the non-renewable oil resources of the country is the result of the interplay of both Laws. A series of agreements between the Government and the operating oil companies have also been concluded on related matters, such as the methods of calculation of royalty payments by means of reference crude oils produced outside Venezuela. Later legislation development and contractual arrangements in the oil workers' unions have been covered with particular care.

I have confined myself to reporting sketchily on new principles or the most radical and meaningful changes introduced as petroleum legislation evolved. It would, no doubt, have been out of place in a chronology to have done otherwise. With regard to the collective contracts signed between the oil workers' unions and the operating oil companies, I have shown the date of the signing of the first of such contracts; in practice, exactly similar documents are signed within a very short period of time between the unions and each of the petroleum companies in the country.

A natural tendency of nationalistic pride is the reporting of *firsts*, "the largest", "the biggest", and similar events. The oil industry of Venezuela can rightly claim many world records. I have reported them but within the shades of grey the chronicle gives; a fact which is certainly not going to deter anyone wishing to boast about an occurrence, from quoting it from its proper place in this book.

Procedures in Venezuela with respect to legal matters do not vary considerably from those of most other countries: the National Congress promulgates a law, which comes into force following signature by the Head of State, whereupon it is published in the official gazette. The first date is given in this book, although I am sorry to report that eminent lawyers whom I have consulted have sometimes disagreed, for reasons unknown to me, on the date of particularly well-known and widely quoted laws. Resolutions issued by a Ministry, or Presidential Decrees, are generally published in the official gazette on the day they are issued, which simplifies matters.

Not all the events which the reader might wish to see in this Chronology have been included. This is, of course, unfair but I have had to apply strict criteria in the selection of events. I have endeavoured to record all those significant to the development of the industry, those which were influential in shaping up future policy or which precipitated further action. But, particularly with reference to more recent history, there might be diversity of opinion on the inclusion of an occurrence, or on the omission of another, no matter how careful I have been in assessing a certain trend, or in foreseeing as reasonably as possible the significance of an event a few years hence. It is just a question of ripening with time.

Social and economic conditions in Venezuela have greatly influenced events, as is true of all nations in the process of development. Purely political matters are not mentioned, but I have certainly included important national events. Governmental policies are covered. In this respect it will be noticeable that reference to them has acquired a tangible character over the last decade, quite different from that of any previous year or period. The key figures in the development of those policies emerge naturally and effortlessly even from the flattened-out entries of the Chronology. Policies of private operating companies have been indicated in the rare instances when they were self-evident or made public knowledge.

Since the late forties, Venezuela has been active in international oil relations and so naturally I have given special attention to important developments connected with those actions, which for one thing resulted in the establishment in September of 1960 of the Organisation of the Petroleum Exporting Countries. In OPEC, Venezuela and other important oil exporters with fundamentally similar interests and objectives are working together for the unification of their petroleum policies, determined to best safeguard their interests—due regard being given to the necessity of investors in the industry securing a fair return on their capital, and consuming countries obtaining an efficient and economic flow of oil.

Events leading to the establishment of the Latin American State Oil Companies' Mutual Assistance Association—ARPEL—and further developments relating to this intergovernmental organization, have also been covered—I hope adequately—as well as the activities in the international scene of the petroleum federation of workers.

To a limited degree, I have also recorded outstanding international events which had direct bearing on national developments; for instance, the expropriation decree of Mexican President Cárdenas, or the nationalization carried out by Mossadegh. In particular, I have covered those actions in the United States, and other countries consuming Venezuelan oil, which have posed difficult problems for it, as in the case of the voluntary, later mandatory, imports control programme of the U.S. Included also in the Chronology are international events with

14

world-wide implications, such as the assassination of Archduke Franz Ferdinand in Sarajevo or the invasion of South Korea.

The first reference to Venezuelan oil dates back to 1535. It is a pity that it was totally wrong. Fernández de Oviedo y Valdés was known to have recorded what was said to him with complete disregard for exactitude; he reported an oil seepage which never existed, accrediting Cubagua with a deposit of the substance which was, in reality, found abundantly nearby on the mainland. Cubagua was, at the time, a coveted island—because of the pearl fisheries of Margarita island. For the sake of fairness I must say that in 1540, when Fernández published the second part of his *Hystoria,* he gave an accurate reference to the seepages which border Lake Maracaibo. Why it should have happened that, adding insult to injury, each successive historian repeated once and again the incorrect occurrence of oil in Cubagua rather than the exact one of Maracaibo, is beyond comprehension. (As a curiosity, I wish to add that this unfortunate error was given, *in 1957,* as the "proof" of the existence of hydrocarbons reservoirs in Cubagua by someone who published his article in the house-organ of an oil company operating in Venezuela for years.)

Humboldt was the first to give us, during the first decade of the nineteenth century, a scientific report on the physiography and geological setting of Venezuela, including, of course, fairly complete references to the natural occurrences of hydrocarbons and thermal springs in the country. Literature on the subject grew considerably after publication in 1841 of the three-volume book on the physical and economic geography of Venezuela by Col. Codazzi, mainly, through the studies and reports of German-speaking naturalists and geologists. Emphasis was given at the time, quite naturally, to the asphalt deposits.

As the current century progressed, the geological knowledge of the Venezuelan basins grew, although little of real importance was published excepting a huge and inaccurate book by Liddle (1928). It was at least two decades before basic papers for the understanding of the petroleum geology of the country were made public at the Geological Congresses of 1937 and 1938, putting an end to the unreasonable policy of non-publication and secrecy among

15

operators due to "competitiveness". The Venezuelan State oil agency has introduced now a new dimension into the picture, as shown by the reports the CVP submitted to the 7th World Petroleum Congress on the Gulf of Venezuela basin, the tar sands belt and the progress of exploration in the Guanarito area.

Six months after the first Mining Code was promulgated, abrogating the *Ordenanzas* de Aranjuez, a concession for the exploitation of asphalt deposits was granted to a certain D.B. Hellyer in September 1854. The first oil concession in Venezuela was the one granted in 1865 by the constitutional President of Zulia State. The concessionaire could drill, produce and export petroleum and naphtha, "or whatever the name of the oil which exists in the earth". The concession should have lasted ten years, but was cancelled in less than one, due to non-compliance with the provisions in the contract.

A decade later, that is, only twenty years after the "Drake" well adventure, Venezuela had its first commercial petroleum company, the Compañía Nacional Petrolia del Táchira. As I have said elsewhere, the importance of Petrolia is not merely historical, nor was the establishment of the company a romantic event devoid of consequences. Petrolia was truly Venezuelan; it was an integrated company which actually competed favourably for years with foreign concerns which claimed to possess, exclusively, the "know-how".

I greatly enjoyed undertaking this self-imposed task. Even to the risk of prolixity, I have recorded the purely curious—the *Leona* field was discovered by the *Tigre* wildcat—and the grotesque, together with the historical occurrence and the overall important event. (It had to be that way.) At the end I came to agree that history, as has been said so often, repeats itself. To us today it might seem that the year of decision for the petroleum industry in Venezuela was 1966, with the introduction of reference prices, the amendment of the income tax law and the strengthening of the CVP, among other events; problems in the past were equally as decisive for the people who had to cope with them. Some in Venezuela claim for new concessions; this also has happened in the past whenever the concessionare companies considered that, to safeguard their interests, they needed more leases. Others indignantly demand an end to the exploitation of our resources by greedy foreigners, as has been done so many times. When the Government tried recently to introduce a tax on the dividends of the operating companies, a number of uninformed people turned in rage towards a particular person, or to OPEC. They did not know their history because in the twenties, Torres—on that occasion also unsuccessfully—tried to include such a provision in the bitterly attacked Law which was finally passed on June 30, 1920.

A final word. I have given in the Chronology such additional information as I considered relevant to allow proper identification of producing areas or fields. The location is shown in a standardized form within brackets. The start of drilling operations—in oilfield terminology, spudding in—of an important or meaningful well is sometimes given, i.e., Oficina-1, Lama-1. A number of appendixes and figures have been included after the chronological section for the benefit of the readers. The figures are self-explanatory. The location of the fields is shown in alphabetical order in one appendix, the fields in the Oficina group in another. Other tables show the oilfields by discovery year, the area under concession or assignment, data on refineries and pipelines, production and exports, the twenty largest fields on account of the volume of their estimated resources, and the twenty fields which have produced the largest amounts of oil at year-end 1966. One appendix lists the internal consumption of products in the domestic markets and another, financial data on the industry. In the reference section at the end of the book, I have listed the most important sources I have consulted in the preparation of this Chronology, from which material was used or which served for checking data and information; but it might happen that I missed some, unintentionally. I have arranged the list by years and by subjects, in a way which I hope should improve its usefulness to the reader.

CHRONOLOGY

In early pre-Discovery days the Indians were well aware of the conspicuous natural surface occurrences of hydrocarbons which exist in Venezuela. Of course, they could not realize that one day the substance they used for their medicines and illuminations was to become known as oil and could swing the balance of world economics and politics. The Indians used the word *mene,* which in fact is still in use today for the seepages they had discovered. Together with these seepages, the Indians found the asphalt, which they used for caulking their canoes and impregnating the sails of their boats, and the pitch, which they used for lining their hand-woven baskets. They hunted deer and other wild animals in and around the seepages (turned into excellent trapping grounds by the heat of the sun). In what is today Trujillo State, the Indians collected lighter oils from along the small creeks near the seepages by impregnating blankets and then wringing them out.

1128

The *Fuero Viejo de Castilla* declares that no one could work mines in the "land property of the King".

1499-1528

The Spanish conquerors are greatly impressed with the natural occurrences of hydrocarbons in Venezuela. They learn from the Indian *piaches* to use the substances for medicinal purposes; they also used them for caulking their ships, for illumination and for treating their weapons.

1535

September

Gonzalo Fernández de Oviedo y Valdés, in his *General and Natural History of the Indies* (*Historia General y Natural de las Indias, Islas y Tierra-Firme del Mar Oceano*), is first to mention Venezuelan oil seepages. He reports an "abundant" seep at the western end of Cubagua island. The "nectar from Cubagua" is very useful for many things and for various sicknesses, in particular gout and others due to coolness, he said. Some had called the substance *stercus demonis*.

1536

September 3

The Queen of Spain, Joanna, in a letter from Valladolid to "the officials who send of the oil petroleum" (*azeite petrolio*) from Nueva Cádiz, Cubagua, orders that "as much of it as possible be sent to me in all ships coming from said Island". The Queen mentions "a fountain" of oil in Cubagua and that all the amounts already sent "had seemed to be of good".

1539

April 30

One barrel of Venezuelan oil is sent to Spain in the *nao* "Santa Cruz", Mestre Francisco Rodríguez de Covarrubia and Captain Bernardino de Fuentes, by Don Francisco de Castellanos, Treasurer of Nueva Cádiz, "to alleviate the gout of Emperor Charles V". This is the first documented shipment of petroleum from Venezuela.

October 18

Following the arrival in Spain of the *nao* "Santa Cruz," the Queen sends a letter from Madrid to the House of Trade (*Casa de Contratación*) in Seville requesting that the "barrel of oil petroleum" be forwarded to her.

October 31
The barrel of oil is sent by the *Casa de Contratación* to the Queen in Madrid in the custody of Alfonso García, a muleteer (*arriero*) from Cuerva.

1540

In Second Part of his *General and Natural History of the Indies*, Gonzalo Fernández de Oviedo y Valdés, reports on the occurrence of many oil seepages (*ojos ò manantiales de betun*) in the Gulf of Venezuela area, "which the Indians call *mene*". He says some seeps are "one-quarter of a league in circumference".

December 14
Another barrel of oil from Venezuela is known to have arrived at the *Casa de Contratación* in Seville. It is to be forwarded to the Queen "in the custody of person of responsibility". This is probably one of the last oil shipments through Cubagua, as an earthquake destroyed Nueva Cádiz and all other settlements in the Island on Christmas Day, 1541.

1551

December 17
By Royal Declaration it is established that, like the Spaniards, Indians can discover, own and work mines.

1552

Francisco López de Gomara, in his *General History of the Indies* (*Historia General de las Indias*), repeating Fernández de Oviedo y Valdés, refers to a seepage in Cubagua and the corresponding stain in the neighbouring sea.

1579

Mayor Gaspar de Párraga y Rodríguez de Argüelles of Maracaibo reports of an oil seepage near the city of Nueva Zamora (Maracaibo) and four more "in the province". They also give a detailed description of how the oil is used locally.

1589

Juan de Castellanos, in his *Elegies* (*Elegías de Varones Ilustres de Indias*), refers to a "fountain" seepage in Cubagua. He says the "proven and excellent liquor" is commonly used for medicinal purposes. When the sea currents are strong, oil stains extend for "three leagues" in the sea.

1602

The *Leyes de Indias* authorize the Royal Governors to apply the laws of Spain throughout the American Colonies.

1626

December 9
Charles I issues a Royal Edict on Mining.

1641-1678

French and English buccaneers, who roamed the Caribbean in their anti-Spanish piratical adventures, enter Lake Maracaibo, chiefly by force, to repair their sea-battered ships with pitch from the many seepages bordering the lake. Gerard, Jackson (twice), Montbars, Nau, Morgan and Granmont sacked Maracaibo or Gibraltar (at the south end of the lake); Granmont went as far inland as Trujillo.

1680

May 18

Charles II publishes a *Recopilación de Indias* containing all previous legal references to mines and mining.

1730

Antonio Herrera refers to the "fountain of smelly medicinal liquor" in Cubagua in his *General History* (*Historia General de los hechos de los Castellanos en las islas i Tierra Firme del Mar Oceano*).

1783

May 22

Charles III of Spain dictates the Mining Ordinances for New Spain (*Ordenanzas de Minería para la Nueva España*) at Aranjuez. Mines are declared the property of the Royal Crown; the King can grant mining concessions. Disposition 22, Sixth Title, specifies "any other fossils, be they perfect or semi-minerals, bitumens, or juices of the earth".

1784

April 27

By Royal Resolution and Royal *Cédula*, the *Ordenanzas de Minería* of Aranjuez are applied to the Intendency of Venezuela.

1791

Joseph Gumilla, in his *Natural, Civil and Geographical History of the Orinoco Region* (*Historia Natural, Civil y Geográfica de las naciones situadas en las riberas del Río Orinoco*), reports on the use of pitch from Trinidad, mostly for medicinal purposes.

1799

July 16

Naturalists Alexander von Humboldt and Aimé Bonpland arrive in Venezuela (Cumaná).

1806

F. Depons, in his *Voyage à la partie orientale de la Terre Firme, dans l'Amérique Méridionale, fait pendant les années 1801, 1802, 1803 et 1804,* refers to oil seeps to the northeast of Lake Maracaibo, near a place called *Mena* (?), and concludes that vapours emanating from them are the cause of the "Catatumbo lightning" (which is a purely atmospherical phenomenon).

1807

Humboldt gives the first serious account of the asphalt deposits in Venezuela in his *Travels to the Equinoctial Regions of America* (*Reise in die Aequinoctial-Gegenden des neuen Continents in den Jahren 1799, 1800, 1801, 1802, 1803 und 1804*). He relates the deposits to the causes which produce earthquakes and eruptions of lava in northern South America. He also described how the natives living near seepages used the pitch and the asphalt. Humboldt gives a list of the natural occurrences of hydrocarbon and hot springs from Trinidad to Maracaibo.

1813

J. J. Dauxion Lavaysse, in his *Trip to Trinidad, Tobago and Margarita Islands* (*Voyage aux Iles de Trinidad, de Tabago, de la Marguerite et dans diverses parties de Vénézuéla, dans l'Amérique Méridionale*), refers to seeps near Cumaná and Barcelona.

1825

Samples of light oil from a seepage reportedly located between Escuque and Betijoque are sent to the United Kingdom, France and the United States.

1829

October 24

Simón Bolívar dictates *Reglamento sobre Minas* decree in Quito, reiterating national ownership of "mines of all kinds".

1830

Group from El Moján (near Maracaibo) explores the Sierra de Perijá area (Socuy river). A burning gas seepage (believed by them to be a volcano) frightens them.

1832

April 29

Venezuelan Congress ratifies Bolívar decree dictated in Quito, on national ownership of "mines of all kinds". Applicability of the *Ordenanzas de Minería* of Aranjuez also accepted.

1839

October 3

Dr. José María Vargas reports to the Ministry of Finance on a sample of asphalt sent to him. He refers to its occurrence in Venezuelan soil and to the fact that he already had "a bottle of this oil brought from the Trujillo Province". He proposes further investigation to determine a real extent, form of occurrence and depth of deposit, "daring to consider" that the State might even grant concessions for exploitation of the resource. The sample had been collected at Pedernales, Lower Orinoco canton.

1841

Agustín Codazzi refers to "fountains of oil" near Trujillo and Cumaná, and to asphalt deposits in Mérida, Coro and Maracaibo, in his "Summary of the Geography of Venezuela".

1849

May 3
A small quake, felt in Maracaibo, is associated with the Perijá "volcano".

1850

First summary of geology of central and eastern Venezuela is published by Hermann Karsten in Journal of German Geological Society (*Zeit. der Deutschen geol. Ges.*). The accompanying map shows the location of numerous hot springs.

1852

Karsten reports from Barranquilla (on September 20) that petroleum seepages can be found in many places all around Lake Maracaibo.

1853

Karsten refers in an article on Venezuelan geology, published in the Karsten Archiv (Berlin), to an oil seep between Escuque and Betijoque (*Bottijoque*).

1854

March 15
First Venezuelan Mining Code (*Código de Minas*) is enacted, abrogating *Ordenanzas de Aranjuez*.

September 6
A concession for the exploitation of asphalt is granted to D. B. Hellyer.

1855

The area west of Lagunillas (Zulia) is explored. Burning gas and oil seepages are related to volcanic activity.

January 4
Presidential Decree of José Gregorio Monagas contains Regulations for 1854 Mining Code. Article 2 establishes need of concessions to exploit combustible deposits, which are the property of the State.

1857

May 6
A Development Board (*Junta de Hacienda*) asks permission from the President of Zulia to exploit the asphalt in the State and that no contracts be given to the private persons which have asked for them.

1858

Oil industry first production. James Miller Williams began producing oil from shallow holes dug at Oil Springs, Ontario, Canada.

1859

August 27
"Colonel" Drake completes first oil well in the United States.

1860

May 16
In a report read to the Geological Society of London, G. P. Wall refers to mineral pitch "extensively diffused in the province of

Maturín . . . and in still larger quantities near the Gulf of Maracaybo" and to mud volcanoes near Maturín (locations shown in accompanying map).

1864

April 13
Federal Constitution transfers to State property of petroleum and combustibles.

1865

August 24
General Jorge Sutherlan, Constitutional President of Zulia State, grants the first oil concession in Venezuela to Camilo Ferrand, an American. The lease covered the State for a duration of ten years; Ferrand could drill, produce and export (*taladrar, sacar y exportar*) petroleum or naphtha—"or whatever the name is of the oil which exists in the earth". A royalty of five pesos per ton was fixed, although the State could request for payments of 20,000 pesos at agreed intervals. The State did not exempt Ferrand of the payment of duties for importing the machinery needed for the operations. The concession contract lapsed before a year.

1866

February 2
The legislature of Nueva Andalucía State (now Sucre and Monagas) grants an oil concession to Manuel Olavarría. The lease covered the whole State for twenty-five years; a royalty of 17% was fixed and Sr. Olavarría had to carry out certain improvements to the cities of Cumaná and Maturín at his own expense.

December 19
The Constitutional Assembly of Trujillo State grants a concession near Escuque for a duration of twenty years.

28

1867

May

Adolf Ernst creates the Caracas Society for Natural and Physical Sciences.

1869

April 12-14

Arístides Rojas publishes a three-article series in *La Opinión Nacional*, referring to the line of hot springs, asphalt deposits and seepages in northeastern Venezuela and Trinidad (Chapapote— Mexican word for *mene*, Aragua, Chaguaramal, Araya, mouth of Guarapiche).

1870

Rojas, in a book on the geography of Venezuela, gives numerous references to asphalt deposits and petroleum seepages.

1873

A report in the bulletin of the Ministry of Development refers to asphalt and petroleum "mines" in Trujillo (near Escuque), Falcón and Araya (near Cariaco Gulf).

1874

Ernst establishes chair of Natural History at the Central University of Caracas.

1875

In a book published in Paris (*Venezuela Pintoresca e Ilustrada*) Miguel Tejera refers to two known "mines" of petroleum in Trujillo (Escuque), and many more in Falcón and in Araya. He also refers to abundant asphalt deposits: "mines" near Gibraltar, Altagracia (Zulia), Guanoco and "inexhaustible" deposits in Mérida.

29

May 18
Cúcuta (Colombia) earthquake. In Venezuela, some thirty kms. to the southeast, in the coffee plantation of Don Manuel Antonio Pulido, sticky oil starts oozing out of a large fracture. He commences the promotion of a company to exploit the deposit.

1876

February 8
In an official (anonymous) report to the President of the Zulia State, "asphalt and *mene* mines" in the Misoa, Cabimas and Perijá areas are discussed.

June 30
Ing. Gen. Wenceslao Briceño Méndez submits to President of Zulia very accurate and complete report on the petroleum and asphalt deposits in the Maracaibo basin: west of Maracaibo, Perijá, Río de Oro, Tarra, eastern shores of the lake. He refers to an oil seep in Tarra producing at a rate 5,760 gal. per day.

1878

September 3
Pulido secures from the government of the Gran Estado de Los Andes (Táchira) exclusive rights to exploit a 100 hectare parcel fifteen kilometres west of San Cristóbal, near Rubio.

October 12
Pulido and associates establish the Compañía Nacional Minera Petrolia del Táchira.

1879

Pedro Rafael Rincones, one of the partners of Pulido, travels to Pennsylvania to study the oil industry.

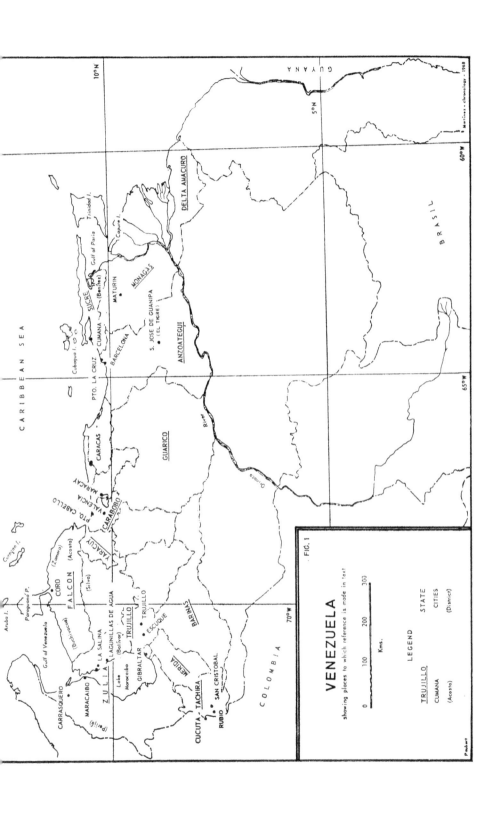

VENEZUELA

showing places to which reference is made in text

0	100	200	300

Kms.

LEGEND

TRUJILLO	STATE
CUMANA	CITIES
(Acosta)	(District)

FIG. 1

Martinez - chronology - 1968

CARIBBEAN SEA

COLOMBIA

BRASIL

GUYANA

10°N

5°N

70°W

65°W

60°W

DELTA AMACURO

MONAGAS

ANZOATEGUI

GUARICO

SUCRE

FALCON

CORO

ZULIA

MERIDA

TACHIRA

BARINAS

TRUJILLO

YARACUY

CARABOBO

MARACAY

CARACAS

BARCELONA

CUMANA

MATURIN

PTO. LA CRUZ

S. JOSE DE GUANIPA
(EL TIGRE)

Orinoco River

Gulf of Paria

Trinidad I.

Capure I.

Cubagua I.

(Benitez)

(Zamora)

(Acosta)

(Silva)

(Bolivar)

(Buchivacoa)

(Perija)

PTO. CABELLO

VALENCIA

MARACAIBO

Lake
Maracaibo

GIBRALTAR

ESCUQUE

LAGUNILLAS DE AGUA

LA SALINA

TRUJILLO

SAN CRISTOBAL

RUBIO

CUCUTA

Gulf of Venezuela

Paraguana P.

Aruba I.

Curacao I.

Margarita I.

1880

A drilling rig is shipped from Pennsylvania to La Alquitrana, the concession site of Petrolia. In the meantime, shallow pits had been dug and petroleum was scooped out with buckets or, Indian fashion, wrung out of impregnated clothes.

French chemist J. B. J. D. Boussingault reports on his research concerning in particular on the composition of Venezuelan thermal waters and the geographic distribution of natural asphalt.

1881

April 27
New Constitution declares that although States are owners, administration of mines rests with the Federal Government.

1882

A teapot-like still with a 600-gallon daily capacity was set up by Petrolia in La Alquitrana, not very far from the producing area. Drilling continues; one well, apparently named Eureka, reached 125 feet total depth.

August 1
Petrolia is legally constituted. Carlos González Bona is appointed President.

1883

March 3
First Law—Decree on mining referring to the 1881 Constitution is published.

May 5
A concession to exploit the Guanoco asphalt lake is granted to Horacio R. Hamilton and Jorge A. Philips.

November 15
Second Law—Decree on mining referring to the 1881 constitution is issued. The duration of the mining concession is fixed at no more than 99, no less than 50 years.

1884

A concession to exploit oil and other minerals is granted to Sixto González, covering part of the Guárico State.

March 25
A concession for 99 years to exploit oil and asphalt, covering part of the Zulia State, is granted to José Andrade of Maracaibo.

April 17
The Andrade concession is amended, to exclude exploitation of asphalt.

August 13
A concession for 20 years is granted to Cristóforo Dacovich covering parts of the Andes and Falcón States, to exploit and refine oil.

October
Wilhelm Sievers arrives in Venezuela.

1885

May 23
A new Mining Code (*Código de Minas*) and ordinance is issued.

November
Sievers ends his Venezuelan trip.

1886

New York and Bermúdez Co., subsidiary of General Asphalt, succeeds in acquiring the Hamilton concession to develop the asphalt lake near Guanoco.

1887

May 30
A short six article Mining Code is passed. For the first time reference is made to mineral substances—coal, asphalt, bitumen.

August 3
Regulations to the Mining Code (*Decreto Reglamentario*) are enacted. The long decree defines for the first time "soil" and "subsoil".

1888

Sievers lists and describes fifty-seven hot springs sites in Venezuela.

May 12
Charles Bullman writes in the Engineering and Mining Journal (New York) about the large asphalt deposits discovered in the delta of the Orinoco. He also reports that "petroleum of superior quality is found in Tachira".

1889

September 8
Ernst writes about the geological evolution of Lake Maracaibo and nearby oil occurrences.

1890

Graham Company of Trinidad drills four shallow wells at La Brea, Capure Island, near Pedernales. The project is later abandoned.

1891

June 26
A new Mining Code (*Código de Minas*) is issued.

July 4
First issue of Bulletin of Public Resources (*Boletín de la Riqueza Pública*) includes table showing asphalt deposits in many localities in Venezuela, also listing a "very active oil seep" in El Infierno (Zulia) and Pedernales asphalt deposit "under exploitation".

September 12
Regulations on the latest Mining Code are published.

September 19
Bulletin of Public Resources reports 4,316 Kg. of asphalt were exported during 1890.

1892

January 9
Bulletin of Public Resources reports Andrés E. Level owns asphalt mines in Orinoco delta area "considered excellent by Dr José María Vargas".

1893

March 29
Another *Código de Minas* is passed.

1894

July 15
An article in *El Cojo Ilustrado* reports gas and electricity displaces usage of petroleum products for illumination in Caracas. Predictions are attempted concerning the development of the oil industry in Venezuela.

1895

E. Fortin reports to the Geographical Society (Paris) on the Guanoco asphalt lake.

1896

H. Eggers publishes a paper on the asphalt deposits of the Lake Maracaibo area.

1898

Wilhelm Sievers reports on the trips made during March of 1892 and 1893 by chem. Richard Ludwig to El Hervidero mud volcano, southeast of Maturín.

Clifford Richardson makes detailed report on the "Bermudez" asphalt lake (Guanoco).

1899

October 22

Gen. Cipriano Castro occupies Caracas and takes over power. During his administration, first important concessions are granted.

1900

The Val de Travers Asphalt Paving Co., an English concern, begins exploiting asphalt in the Pedernales area. A small asphalt refinery was erected.

A concession is granted to the United States and Venezuela Co. (Uvalde Asphalt Paving Co.), to exploit the Inciarte asphalt lake, Zulia State. The company operated for four years; a small asphalt refinery was built at Carrasquero. In 1905, the Government took the concession back.

New York and Bermúdez Co. begins exploitation of the asphalt deposits in the Guanoco lake. The mineral is exported to Brazil.

An Italian engineer, E. Cortese, reports on asphalt deposits and oil seeps of Venezuela at Guanoco and Guariquen, Putucual, east end of Cariaco gulf, Manicuare, Maracaibo area and "near Puerto Cabello".

1903

L. Hirzel writes about the petroleum and asphalt deposits in the delta of the Orinoco river (Pedernales, Plata island).

1904

January 23
A new Mining Code (*Código de Minas*) is issued, abrogating the Code of 1893.

May 16
A 1,214-hectare concession is granted to Andrés Espina and others in Perijá and Maracaibo areas.

A contract for the exploitation of asphalt mines in Perijá and Maracaibo is concluded between the Federal Executive and Andrés Valbuena and Federico Bohórquez.

1905

Clifford Richardson publishes in London report on Venezuelan asphalts ("Bermudez" and "Maracaibo"), including chemical composition, characteristics and location maps.

August 14
Pres. Castro issues a Mining Law (*Regimen de la Ley de Minas*) under which many of the famous petroleum concessions of Venezuela were to be granted. An annual surface tax of $0.60 per

hectare was established, plus a royalty of $1.20 per ton; concessions could be granted for fifty years and exploitation had to start within four years. Disputes were subject only to Venezuelan law and courts.

December 16
A fifty-year lease is given to Eduardo Echenagucia García covering the Zulia State for the exploitation of oil. The concession was later annulled because work did not start within the time limit.

1906

February 23
The Regulations to the 1905 Law are issued. The executive has the absolute power to grant and administer all concessions without consent of the National Congress.

March 26
The Federal Court (*Corte Federal y de Casación*) recognises the *Ordenanzas de Mineria* of Aranjuez had indeed applied legally to Venezuela.

1907

January 31
A concession is granted for fifty years to Andrés Jorge Vigas in the Río de Oro area. It is later transferred to Colón Development.

February 28
Antonio Aranguren receives a special concession to exploit asphalt in the Bolívar District, Zulia State; concession also covers Maracaibo District.

March 18
A concession is granted to Francisco Jiménez Arráiz for the exploitation of asphalt, pitch and tar in the Acosta and Zamora Districts of Falcón State and the Silva District of Lara State.

July 3
The Jiménez Arráiz concession in Falcón and Lara is amended to also include exploitation of oil. The lease was later transferred to North Venezuelan Petroleum.

July 22
Gen. Bernabé Planas is granted a concession for the exploitation of asphalt, bitumen, pitch and petroleum in the Buchivacoa District of the Falcón State. It is later transferred to British Controlled Oilfields.

August 1
Rafael Gutieri receives a concession for the exploitation of asphalt, bitumen, pitch and petroleum in the Puerto Cabello District of Carabobo State.

1908

Richardson publishes book on "The Modern Asphalt Pavement" (London), pages 178-192 devoted to Venezuela. He gives detailed data on the "Bermudez", "Maracaibo", Inciarte and La Paz asphalts, as well as general information on the exploitation of the deposits.

December 19
Less than a month after the departure of Pres. Castro to Europe, Gen. Juan Vicente Gómez seizes power.

1909

G. Delgado Palacios reports on the various types of naturally occurring hydrocarbons in Venezuela.

April 12
Eloy Escobar Llamosas receives 25-year concession to exploit asphalt in Maturín area.

August 16
A greatly improved Mining Code (*Código de Minas*) is issued.

December 4
A concession covering the Inciarte asphalt lake is granted to E. Stanley Simmons.

December 10
A concession, covering 27 million hectares, is granted to John Allen Tregelles, representative of a British company. It had for the first time a provision promoting local refining of oil produced and another permitting the expropriation for right of way.

1910

L. V. Dalton, in a paper published in London on the geology of Venezuela, refers to the petroleum seepages and oil possibilities in the country.

June 29
A new Mining Code (*Código de Minas*) is enacted.

July 14
Rafael Max Valladares, attorney for General Asphalt, receives a petroleum concession covering the Benítez District of Sucre State (Guanoco pitch lake included). In 1912 the first oil well in Venezuela is drilled under this lease by New York and Bermúdez Co.

August 27
National Congress elects Gen. Gómez as Constitutional President for four years.

February 11
The Inciarte asphalt lake in Zulia State is leased for exploitation to Gen. José María García.

July
One well is drilled near Cumaná by Venezuelan Oil Fields Exploration in the Tragelles concession.

September
Ralph Arnold and his associates start one of the most ambitious exploration programmes in the world, the systematic and scientific study of the oil possibilities of General Asphalt holdings in Venezuela (an area of more than 50 million hectares).

November
Caribbean Petroleum is incorporated in New Jersey by General Asphalt, to hold the concession being negotiated in Venezuela.

December
The Tragelles concession is taken back at end of the prospecting period.

1912

Book on *Venezuela* is published in London by L. V. Dalton, containing throughout references to oil and asphalt industry. Dalton reports the "desultory and ill-advised" attempt to develop asphalt production at Pedernales and the satisfactory exploitation of oil by Petrolia. He remarks that Venezuela should be considered among the important oil-producing countries of the world.

January 2
Valladares receives a concession covering roughly the same area granted to Tragelles, that is, all the Anzoátegui, Carabobo, Táchira, Monagas, Mérida, Lara, Trujillo and Yaracuy States, the Fed. Territory Delta Amacuro plus parts of the States of Zulia, Falcón and Sucre.

January 4
Valladares transfers his concession to Caribbean Petroleum.

June 18
Terms of the Aranguren concession are amended to include right of petroleum exploitation. Five years later, the Bolívar Coastal field is to be discovered under this lease.

August
Bababui-1 is started by Bermúdez Asphalt.

November 27
Arnold submits his preliminary geological report to Caribbean Petroleum, recommending the selection of eighty-seven lots of 500 hectares each in Monagas, Anzoátegui, Sucre, Nueva Esparta, Falcón, Zulia and Trujillo States. He recommended the immediate drilling of a well in Mene Grande: Zumaque.

December
As a last resort, General Asphalt offers Shell participation in its Venezuelan holdings. Henri Deterding, in "perhaps the most speculative venture of my life", buys a 51 % interest in Caribbean Petroleum for $10 million.

1913

January 17
In a complicated financial deal, Burlington Investment Co. is established, permitting Shell, through Caribbean Petroleum, to acquire control of all petroleum rights in the concessions of General Asphalt (ex-Valladares).

February 1
Caribbean Petroleum starts geological work.

March to June
New York and Bermúdez Co. drills twenty-eight shallow wells in and around the Guanoco asphalt lake, to gain control of the 14,000 hectares area.

August 15
New York and Bermúdez Co. discovers the Guanoco field, on completion of well Bababui-1. This is the first oilfield in Venezuela. The area has now been returned to the Government. The oil is very heavy; a total of sixteen producers were eventually drilled, not counting some twenty holes of less than 100 feet total depth (Maturín basin, 60 km NE of Maturín).

September 3
Venezuelan Oil Concessions obtains the Vigas concession.

October
The Aranguren concession is transferred to Venezuelan Oil Concessions.

1914

January 4
As the exploration period of ex-Valladares second concession expires, Caribbean Petroleum, upon the recommendation of Arnold, claims 1,028 exploitation lots, covering 512,000 hectares, around and near oil seeps.

January 12
Wildcat Zumaque-1 is started in Mene Grande area.

April 15
Caribbean Petroleum discovers the first oilfield of importance in Venezuela, upon successful completion of new field wildcat Zumaque-1 (renamed MG-1). The Mene Grande giant field, the sixth in size so far recognized among the Venezuelan oilfields, produced its first 100 millionth barrel in 1932 (Maracaibo basin, 120 km SE of Maracaibo).

June 28
First World War. Archduke Franz Ferdinand and his wife are assassinated in Sarajevo.

August 1
Regulations to Mining Law (*Decreto Reglamentario de Minas*) are issued.

August 2
Caribbean Petroleum discovers the small Totumo field on completion of new field wildcat Zambapalo-3 (Maracaibo basin, 85 km w of Maracaibo).

September 19
Bacante-1 is abandoned by General Asphalt at 4,247 feet, then the deepest well drilled in Venezuela (Maturín basin, 15 km sw of Guanoco asphalt lake).

1915

Shell acquires management control of Venezuelan Oil Concessions.

June 26
A new Mining Law (*Ley de Minas*) is enacted.

July 28
The Planas concession of Buchivacoa District is transferred to the Venezuelan Falcón Oil Syndicate.

September 23
Orden-1 is successfully completed by Colón Development as the discovery well of the small Río de Oro field (Maracaibo basin, 225 km sw of Maracaibo, just north of the Colombian border).

1916

May 8
Regulations to the 1915 Mining Law are issued.

July 25
Arnold ends his work in Venezuela.

August 27
Colón Development discovers the Las Cruces giant oilfield, on completion of new field wildcat Toldo-1, renamed T-1 (Maracaibo basin, Tarra group of fields, 255 km sw of Maracaibo, near Colombian border).

1917

January
Two parallel 10-mile long, 8-inch pipelines from the Mene Grande field to San Lorenzo are put into operation.

June 26
The Shops and Public Establishments Law is passed. This is the first move towards regulating working conditions and workers' rights in Venezuela.

August 17
First refining operations are carried out at the San Lorenzo refinery.

September
First exports of Venezuelan oil by Caribbean Petroleum from the San Lorenzo terminal.

December 13
Venezuelan Oil Concessions successfully completes wildcat Santa Bárbara-1 (renamed R-2). With this completion in the La Rosa area, VOC had unknowingly discovered the Bolívar Coastal field, the largest petroleum accumulation in the world. Resources of the field are estimated at 16,500 million barrels of oil (Maracaibo basin; the area is located 40 km SE of Maracaibo, near Cabimas, on the eastern shore of the lake).

1918

A new Mining Law (*Regimen de la Ley de Minas*) is enacted. It declares that the granting of a concession does not confer owner-

45

ship of the deposit, but only the right to exploit the substance. Four articles deal exclusively with petroleum, incorporating the ideas of Development Minister, Gumersindo Torres. Duration of titles was set at thirty years, surface rentals varied in accordance with producing rates, and royalty was fixed at between 8 and 15 % depending on the distance between the reservoirs and shipping terminals. Areas not in exploitation have to be returned to the Government within three years. First reference made to conservation measures.

October 9
A regulatory decree of the 1918 Mining Law (*Decreto reglamentario del carbón, petróleo y sustancias similares*) is passed. One provision establishes that concessionaires can only exploit half of the area granted for exploration, the other half must be returned to the State as "national reserve".

December 5
A small oil accumulation is discovered on completion of Misoa-1 (Maracaibo basin, 7 km N of Mene Grande field).

December 31
Petroleum appears for the first time in Venezuelan export statistics: 21,194 metric tons, valued at Bs. 900,000.

1919

Intense competition for concessions develops as Americans are encouraged by the Wilson administration to seek for oil rights. Diplomatic support is given to the oilmen by the Caracas Legation.

1920
January 5
The old Planas concession is now transferred to British Controlled Oilfields (Anglo-Persian).

March 17
A second regulatory decree of the 1918 Mining Law is passed.

March 30
Creole Petroleum, a subsidiary of Standard Oil (New Jersey), is incorporated in Delaware.

May
The United States Minister in Venezuela tries to stop passing of new legislation. In this connection, he visits Pres. Gómez in Maracay.

June 30
First Hydrocarbons Law (*Ley sobre Hidrocarburos y demás minerales combustibles*) of Development Minister Gumersindo Torres, is sanctioned by National Congress. Surface taxes are increased, private landholders get an opportunity to obtain exploration permits on their land, size of concessions is reduced, national reserves are expanded and can only be granted for exploitation, list of duty-free import items is greatly reduced. Article 50 fixed the time for selection of exploitation parcels at three years.

August 11
International Petroleum, an affiliate of Standard Oil (New Jersey), is incorporated in Canada.

1921

Alfredo Jahn publishes a summary of the geological formations in Venezuela (*Esbozo de las formaciones geológicas de Venezuela*).

February 15
Settlement of the important "Vigas concession" case, which might have had far reaching importance concerning the validity of all 1907 leases.

47

May 2
Pedro Vicente Navarro asks for exploration permits in Cubagua Island.

May 3
Caribbean Petroleum obtains compromise on the controversy over the Aranguren concession. Later, for Bs. 10 million, any legal arguments on the Valladares leases are settled and Shell has at the end all its holdings guaranteed at least until 1965.

June 1
More than 2,300 Venezuelans have applied for concessions under Article 8 of the Hydrocarbons Law giving landowners an option for leases on their own property.

June 8
The first oilfield in the Falcón basin, El Mene de Mauroa, is discovered by British Controlled Oilfields, on completion of new field wildcat EM-1 (60 km E of Maracaibo).

June 16
A second Hydrocarbons Law (*Ley sobre Hidrocarburos y demás minerales combustibles*) is enacted. Pres. Gómez, yielding to pressure, had allowed the operating companies to help draw up the Law (Minister Torres had been dismissed earlier). Exploitation area was doubled, royalty was fixed at 10%, in cash or kind. Damage, waste and fires were to be avoided.

December 12
Standard Oil of Venezuela, subsidiary of Standard Oil (New Jersey), is incorporated.

1922

January 22
An exploration concession in Cubagua Island is granted to José María Merchán.

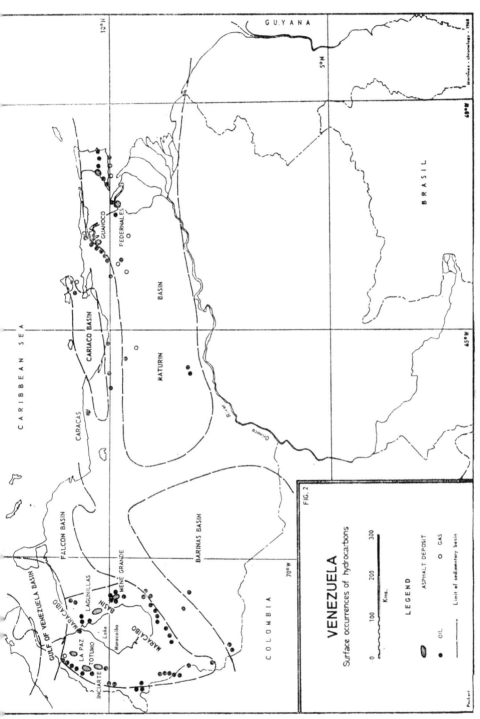

CARIBBEAN SEA

GUYANA

VENEZUELA
Surface occurrences of hydrocarbons

FIG. 2

LEGEND

ASPHALT DEPOSIT

OIL   O GAS   Limit of sedimentary basin

Kms.

0   100   200   300

CARACAS

CARIACO BASIN

GUANOCO

PEDERNALES

MATURIN

BASIN

R. +

Orinoco

FALCON BASIN

GULF OF VENEZUELA BASIN

MARACAIBO

LA PAZ

TOTUMO

INCIARTE

LAGUNILLAS

MENE GRANDE

Lake
Maracaibo

MARACAIBO BASIN

BARINAS BASIN

COLOMBIA

BRASIL

10°N

5°N

68°W

65°W

70°W

D

March
Two shallow-draft lake tankers, able to clear the Maracaibo bar, are put into operation by Caribbean Petroleum.

April 6
Venezuelan Petroleum (Sinclair) is incorporated in Delaware.

June
Pauji-2 of New England Oil near Betijoque, Trujillo State, is completed as a small producer. A Venezuelan company, Minerales Petrolíferos Río Pauji, unsuccessfully tried to develop commercial production in the area by drilling shallow wells close to seepages.

June 9
A third *Ley sobre Hidrocarburos y demás minerales combustibles* is sanctioned by the National Congress. It was a simple, practical document, meant to remove all ambiguities from the 1921 Law. Size of parcels was increased and duration of exploitation extended to forty years. Royalty was to be paid on the basis of the market value at embarkation point. All American leases were converted to this liberal Law, which was to regulate the industry for more than twenty years.

July 27
Standard Oil of Venezuela discovers the small Los Barrosos oilfield on completion of wildcat Barrosos-2 (Maracaibo basin, 5 km N of Mene Grande field).

December 14
Well Los Barrosos-2 (renamed R-4) of the Venezuelan Oil Concessions blows out from 1,500 feet, at an estimated rate of 100,000 barrels per day of 16° API gravity oil (La Rosa area of the Bolívar Coastal field).

December 23
Los Barrosos-2 sands up and stops flowing. Total production during the nine-day blow out is estimated at nearly one million barrels of oil.

February 15
Las Flores-1 (renamed P-3) discovers the La Paz field. The well was completed in shallow Eocene sands (Maracaibo basin, 40 km w of Maracaibo).

March 23
Venezuela Gulf Oil is incorporated.

May 20
A small oil accumulation is discovered at El Menito (Maracaibo basin, 5 km N of Mene Grande field).

June 19
Lago Petroleum starts operations in Venezuela.

June 22
The Compañía Venezolana del Petróleo is incorporated in Caracas. Headed by personal friends of Pres. Gómez, it is the favoured instrument of the Dictator to pursue his policy of disposal of national reserves.

October
Side-stepping Development Minister Antonio Alamo, the United States Minister in Venezuela receives assurances from Pres. Gómez to a prompt and satisfactory solution of the controversy on the Planas concession.

November
First exports of oil from the El Mene de Mauroa field. Oil was moved to a terminal at La Estacada through a 55-km pipeline laid parallel to the company's narrow-gauge railroad.

December 13
Federal Executive gives one-fourth exemption to exploitation tax payments of Mene Grande.

MT-1 discovers first Eocene production in the Mene Grande field.

First geophysical work in Venezuela. It was a short survey by electrical methods, in Western Venezuela.

February
Pres. Gómez announces that the German interests, Stinnes, are willing to buy huge holdings of Compañía Venezolana del Petróleo.

March 26
American Legation in Caracas is instructed to inform the Venezuelan Government about concern of United States if American oilmen are excluded, or discriminated against, on the acquisition of national reserves.

April 22
First well of British Equatorial under waters of Lake Maracaibo.

May
Led by Standard Oil (New Jersey), American companies start buying concessions from the Compañía Venezolana del Petróleo.

June
First oil exports by an American oil company from Venezuela (Lago Petroleum).

August 12
Lago Oil and Transport, a wholly-owned subsidiary of Standard Oil (New Jersey), is incorporated in Canada. It owns and operates the Aruba refinery.

1925

February
A. Hamilton Garner publishes quite complete picture of the oil geology of northern Venezuela.

March
Lago Petroleum completes a small refinery at La Salina (near Cabimas).

May 9
Venezuelan Atlantic Refining is incorporated in Delaware.

June 1
Well R-28 of Venezuelan Oil Concessions blows out and causes furious blaze. Production during the two-day uncontrolled flow is estimated at 100,000 barrels of oil (La Rosa area, Bolívar Coastal field).

June 2
Caribbean Petroleum discovers a small field at La Concepción on completion of shallow well C-2 (Maracaibo basin, 20 km w of Maracaibo).

June 20
Commercial production starts in the La Paz field.

June 24
The Constitution declares that mines are the property of the States, but are administered by the Federal Government.

July
Although not yet properly organized, oil workers strike in the Lake Maracaibo area, protesting against rapidly increasing cost of living. Pres. Gómez sends troops to maintain order. A 20 per cent gain on the fixed one-dollar-a-day wage is nevertheless gained.

July 18
A Hydrocarbons Law, almost identical to that of 1922, is published in the Official Gazette.

December 31
Cumulative production reaches almost 40 million barrels of oil; proved reserves are estimated at 500 million barrels.

A. H. Garner publishes the first correlation chart of the geological formations in Venezuela.

In very long communication to the Officio Geologico d'Italia, E. Fossa Mancini reports on an oil seep near Puerto Cabello (apparently, the same one to which Cortese had referred in his 1901 paper).

January 18
The Ambrosio area of the Bolívar Coastal field opens up on completion of well Rodríguez-2 of Venezuela Gulf.

January 22
Standard Oil of Venezuela discovers the small Monte Claro field; the area is now returned to the National Government; three out of five wells drilled are producers (Falcón basin, 170 km sw of Coro, 40 km e of El Mene de Mauroa field).

March 11
Well Lago-1 of Mene Grande is completed as an oil producer, opening up the Lagunillas area of the Bolívar Coastal field. Although on the basis of an arbitrary nomenclature, Lagunillas is the largest producing area of the BCF.

April
Lago Petroleum acquires the offshore Lake Maracaibo concessions of British Equatorial Oil.

April 13
Very complete report on the oilfields of the Maracaibo basin is presented by C. M. Hunter to the Institution of Petroleum Technologists in London.

August 26
Well Unity-1 of Venezuela Gulf opens up the Punta Benítez area of the Bolívar Coastal field.

October 29
First oil well of Lago Petroleum (LL-2) is completed in the Lagunillas area of the Bolívar Coastal field.

November 12
Coro Petroleum discovers the small Urumaco oilfield on completion of wildcat El Mamón-1A (Falcón basin, 70 km wsw of Coro).

December 31
Petroleum becomes the first export commodity of Venezuela: 3,836,475 metric tons worth Bs. 192 million.

1927

First geophysical survey in Eastern Venezuela: torsion balance, refraction and magnetic.

January 26
Oil companies are ordered not to drill wells closer than 75 metres one from the other. This was meant to alleviate wasteful competitive drilling along the Mene Grande strip in Lake Maracaibo, Bolívar Coastal field.

March 4
The Los Manueles oilfield is discovered by Colón Development on successful completion of new field wildcat TM-1, renamed CM-1 (Maracaibo basin, Tarra group of fields, 15 km N of Las Cruces field).

March 21
North Venezuelan Petroleum discovers the small Mene de Acosta oilfield, the first in the easternmost Falcón basin (150 km SE of Coro).

April
Mene Grande, Caribbean and Standard (Indiana) agree to reduce competitive drilling and discontinue offsetting.

June 24
BCO (British Controlled Oilfields) discovers the small Hombre Pintado field (Falcón basin, 16 km NE of El Mene de Mauroa field).

December 6
L-44 of Lago Petroleum blows out with tremendous force. Derrick is thrown out into lake.

December 15
Sabaneta-2 (renamed Monef-2) of Standard Oil of Venezuela is tested. Although the results are not commercial, it led to the deepening of Moneb-1—discovery well of the Quiriquire field.

1928

First book on the geology of Venezuela is published by R. A. Liddle.

April 27
Venezuelan Gulf discovers the small Amana field (Maracaibo basin, 70 km NW of Maracaibo).

May 9
Lago Petroleum opens up the important Tía Juana area of the Bolívar Coastal field, on completion of wildcat Tía Juana-1.

June
The increasing volume of Venezuelan oil imports begin to disturb American independent producers. Lobbying commences in Washington for a tariff on imports.

June 1
New field wildcat Moneb-1 of Standard Oil of Venezuela, is successfully completed. This is a very important discovery, the first in the Maturín basin of Eastern Venezuela. The Quiriquire giant field, which produced its first 100 millionth barrel during 1938, is, on account of its resources—more than 800 million barrels—the fourth largest in the country (25 km N of Maturín).

June 7
Standard Oil (New Jersey) purchases its first production of Venezuelan oil, by acquiring control of the Creole Syndicate.

The small Las Palmas field is discovered by Standard Oil of Venezuela. The area is now returned to the Government. Of 13 wells drilled, two produce oil and three gas (Falcón basin, 130 km W of Coro, 40 km NE of El Mene de Mauroa).

June 15
The oil town of Lagunillas de Agua, on the eastern shore of Lake Maracaibo, is partially destroyed by oil blaze.

July 18
A new Hydrocarbons Law (*Ley sobre Hidrocarburos y demás minerales combustibles*) is sanctioned by the National Congress.

July 23
First Labour Law enacted. No minimum wage, unions allowed, maximum daily work hours nine. Workers can be fined for spreading Communist propaganda.

December 31
Production for the year surpasses the 100 million barrels mark for the first time.

1929

Lago Petroleum uses wooden and concrete foundations in their Lake Maracaibo wells at depths of 15 metres.

Colón Development completes small refinery at Casigua.

West India Oil—later absorbed by Lago Petroleum—erects small refinery at La Arreaga, Maracaibo.

Compañía Minera Petrolia del Táchira resumes drilling in its La Alquitrana concession. Nine wells are completed in three years, one of them to 400 feet.

January
A small topping plant is completed near Cabimas by Venezuela Gulf.

March 5
First electric well log outside of France is run in VOC's development well R-216, La Rosa area, Bolívar Coastal field. It was a resistivity survey.

April 14
Orinoco Oil (Pure Oil) discovers the small Netick field (Maracaibo basin, 10 km N of La Paz field. Only field in Venezuela named after an oil man).

May 1
The small Media oilfield is discovered by British Controlled Oilfields (Falcón basin, 7 km NE of El Mene de Mauroa).

October 29
Stock market crash in the United States.

November 19
Recently reappointed Development Minister, Gumersindo Torres, increases tax schedule on national reserves by 50%.

December
Oil companies pay twelve-and-a-half million bolívars in back taxes on buoys in the Maracaibo Bar.

December 31
There are over 100 oil companies operating in the country, but only five export significant volumes of oil.

1930

Colón Development completes 145-km pipeline from the Tarra fields to La Solita. At the time, it was the longest in Venezuela.

May 11
Venezuela Gulf abandons Covir-1 at 8,323 feet total depth, then the deepest well in Venezuela (Maracaibo basin, 60 km sw of Maracaibo).

June
Ministry of Development establishes the Technical Office of Hydrocarbons (*Oficina Técnica de Hidrocarburos*).

July
The Government sends a group of Civil Engineers, graduates of the Caracas Central University, to the United States to specialize in oil.

August 8
Regulations (*Reglamento sobre la Ley . . .*) for the 1928 Hydrocarbons Law are issued by Development Minister Torres, to protect in an efficient manner the interests of the Nation in the petroleum industry.

August 22
In a memorandum to the Ministry of Development, oil companies vehemently protest governmental interference as laid out in new Regulations.

September 30
Development Minister Torres informs oil companies that attacks on the Regulations would be tantamount to deny the sovereignty

59

of the country. Certain impractical provisions are removed, but all new procedures on fiscalization and supervision by Government field inspectors are maintained.

November
As activities are drastically reduced, and thousands dismissed, oil workers of Mene Grande try unsuccessfully to strike.

December
Shell announces voluntary decrease in production of around 20%; Mene Grande and Standard (Indiana), of 10%.

December 7
Blow out of wildcat Lagunita-1, of Mene Grande, the first well of the Bachaquero area of the Bolívar Coastal field.

1931

The SP curve of electric logs introduced commercially in Venezuela.

Colón Development completes small Calvario refinery.

March
In order to ease situation around oilfields, National Government offers to transport back to their homes, those dismissed by the operating companies.

March 22
Group of exiled Venezuelans publish intended programme of government. Barranquilla (Colombia) Plan, Item 7, asks for a thorough revision of concessions policy.

April
Mene Grande, Shell and Standard (Indiana) agree to restrict production 15%.

April 24
The Cumarebo oilfield is discovered by Standard Oil of Venezuela (Creole). Although small, it is yet the largest field found in the Falcón basin (30 km E of Coro).

May
Uzcátegui-1, first new field wildcat in the Barinas basin, is abandoned as a dry hole by Sinclair (15 km NW of Barinas).

June
Development Minister Torres, on the basis of transport costs data released by the US Tariff Commission, accuses oil companies of misrepresenting financial information to the Government. For the period February 1927 to January 1931, Standard (Indiana) has to pay 26 million bolívars, Mene Grande 30 million.

August 14
R-4 (Los Barrosos-2) is closed in and later abandoned. Total production during 8 years—not counting the volume produced during the blow out of 1922—was 500,000 barrels of oil.

August
No well completions during the month, an effect of the depression.

September
Pres. Gómez, yielding to pressure, dismisses Minister Torres. Claims for payments due are not pressed.

October 13
Standard Oil of Venezuela inaugurates the Caripito refinery, for many years to be the largest in the country.

1932

Colón Development completes small Rivera refinery (Tarra fields).

May
Standard Oil (New Jersey) buys lake concessions of Standard Oil (Indiana), thus becoming the dominant oil concern in Venezuela.

June 6
US Congress passes a law introducing a crude and fuel oil tariff of $0.21 per barrel and a gasoline tariff of $1.05, for all imports into the United States.

October 25
Atlantic discovers the Pirital field (Maturín basin, Jusepín group, 25 km sw of Jusepín).

November 18
The first electric log in Eastern Venezuela is run in well Q-78, Quiriquire field.

December 31
There are more than 1,000 oil producing wells in the country, for the first time.

1933

Gas injection starts in the Cumarebo field.
Pressure maintenance by gas injection starts in the La Rosa area of the Bolívar Coastal field.

February 23
Oficina-1 spuds in.

April
Lago Petroleum starts using concrete pile foundations for offshore drilling in Lake Maracaibo. Piles are made in a plant in Lagunillas.

April 15
Standard Oil of Venezuela discovers the Orocual field on completion of well Orocual-2 (Maturín basin, 20 km sw of Quiriquire).

September 2

The Pedernales giant oilfield is discovered by Standard Oil of Venezuela (Creole) on completion of new field wildcat Pedernales-2 (Maturín basin, 100 km NNE of Maturín).

U.S. Secretary of Interior announces imports of crude petroleum are to be limited to amount not exceeding the average daily imports during the second half of 1932. Voluntary compliance to the programme is asked.

November 3

A "B/L" agreement is signed by Mene Grande and Standard Oil of Venezuela. No details available.

1934

January 31
Oficina-1 is suspended.

April 8
The Compañía Nacional Minera Petrolia del Táchira ceases operation.

June
Lago Petroleum plants in La Salina start producing steel and concrete piles for well foundations offshore in Lake Maracaibo.

July 25
Pres. Gómez sets up subsidy for agricultural exporters, as bolívar appreciates to a rate of three to one dollar.

August 23
Exchange controls are introduced. By agreement with the Government, oil companies would sell two-thirds of their dollars to Venezuelan banks at Bs. 3.90, one-third to the Government at 3.06.

December 12
Cumulative production reaches 1,000 million barrels of crude oil. Proved reserves stand now at 2,500 million barrels.

1935

May 27
Import quotas introduced in 1933 in the United States end with death of the National Industry Recovery Act. Voluntary restraint on imports continues.

June 17
The National Congress enacts a new Hydrocarbons Law (*Ley sobre Hidrocarburos y demás minerales combustibles*).

July
Socony tries to bid on national reserve lots offered by the Government, but Minister of Development, Cayama Martínez, gives them to Standard Oil (New Jersey) companies.

November 4
Regulations (*Reglamento sobre la Ley . . .*) for the 1935 Hydrocarbons Law are issued.

December 17
Pres. Gómez dies; Gen. Eleazar López-Contreras temporarily assumes executive powers.

1936

First well to drill through the "tar belt" of the southern border of the Maturín basin, La Canoa-1, is completed (145 km sw of Maturín, 50 km n of the Orinoco river).

February 27
Establishment of the first oil workers' union, *Sindicato de Obreros y Empleados Petroleros de Cabimas*.

March 20
Establishment of the Consultative Department for Mining and Geology, ascribed to the Ministry of Development. Dr. S. E. Aguerrevere is appointed first Director of the Department.

April 25
Gen. López-Contreras is elected President of the Republic by the National Congress.

May
Development Minister, Néstor Luis Pérez, announces that concessions will be granted on competitive bidding. Companies raise royalty payments to 15%, offer rental and surface payments ten, fifteen times the minima, agree to pay in bolívars purchased at Bs. 3.06 (not the official fixed rate of Bs. 3.90), and process larger percentages of their output in Venezuela.

June 15-23
Public debate on oil policies in Caracas daily *La Esfera* between Rómulo Betancourt and Alejandro Pietri, lawyer of Standard Oil of Venezuela.

July 14
Arturo Uslar Pietri, in an editorial in the Caracas daily *Ahora*, puts forward the idea that Venezuela needs "to sow the petroleum" —*sembrar el petróleo*.

July 16
The Labour Law is sanctioned. It includes the most advanced principles of modern social law.

July 20
A law is passed concerning pollution of waters by oil.

August 5
A new Hydrocarbons Law (*Ley sobre Hidrocarburos y demás minerales combustibles*) is sanctioned by the National Congress.

Special advantages of a non-monetary nature could be asked for from companies willing to receive concessions.

September 14
Sharp attacks in the newspaper *Crítica* on the "corrupt methods" of Standard Oil (New Jersey) in acquiring Venezuelan concessions and also on the legality of the Valladares lease.

September 15
New field wildcat Temblador-1 (TT-1) of Standard Oil of Venezuela discovers the Temblador giant oilfield (Maturín basin, 100 km s of Maturín).

October
Minister Pérez demands that oil companies clean up the oil-contaminated shores of Lake Maracaibo and that 'company roads' be open to general circulation.

November 7
Wildcat Santa Ana-1 (renamed AM-1) of Mene Grande makes the first discovery of the Anaco group of field (Maturín basin, 50 km sw of Maturín).

December 14
Thriving on the privileges obtained through the new Labour Law, recently established unions call for a general strike. It was successful.

1937

CR-2, at the time the deepest well in the country, is suspended by Shell, at a total depth of 9,031 feet (Maracaibo basin, 190 km sw of Maracaibo, 40 km e of Río de Oro field).

Following discovery and rapid development of Oficina and fields in the central area of Anzoátegui State, El Tigre evolves into an active population centre. In twenty-five years it was to be the second largest town in Eastern Venezuela. Together with nearby El Tigrito, it became known in the fifties as San José de Guanipa.

The Uracoa field is discovered.

January 15
Regulations on the 1936 Hydrocarbons Law are issued (*Reglamento sobre la Ley ...*)

January 22
Pres. López-Contreras decrees an end to the oil workers' strike. Operating companies do not recognize unions nor give basic rights for payment of overtime and vacations to the workers. Government grants a one-bolívar increase in wages.

January 27
Development Minister Pérez again raises a claim for incorrect reporting of transport costs. Standard settles its 26 million bolívar claim for a little more than Bs. 4 million.

January 31
Due to a resolution of the Ministry of Development, the price of kerosene is lowered.

February
On the occasion of the First Venezuelan Geological Congress, the Technical Service of Mining and Geology publishes the first preliminary geological map of Northern Venezuela.

February 15
The First Venezuelan Geological Congress opens in Caracas.

March 12
Work is resumed in wildcat Oficina-1.

March 17
Mene Grande completes Areo-1. This area is now incorporated into the Merey field.

April 14
MG-1 (Merey-1), of Mene Grande, discovers an important oil-field (Maturín basin, 35 km SE of Oficina).

April 22
Standard Oil of Venezuela discovers the Pilón oilfield (Maturín basin, 10 km. S of Temblador).

June 16
Oficina-1, the discovery well of the Oficina field, renamed OG-1, is completed for 1,337 barrels of oil per day. During 1945, this giant oilfield produced its 100 millionth barrel. Oficina is the seventh largest field in Venezuela due to its resources (Maturín basin, 150 km sw of Maturín).

July 27
An investigating commission of the National Congress condemns the practice of companies informing the Government of the names of the 'agitators', causing thirty labour leaders to be expelled from the Lake Maracaibo area.

September 21
Tocuyo Oilfields shuts-in the El Mene de Acosta field.

November 2
New field wildcat Yopales-1 (renamed YS-1) of Mene Grande is successfully completed, discovering a giant oilfield (Maturín basin, Oficina group 20 km. sw of Oficina field).

December 15
Mene Grande and Standard Oil of Venezuela sign an agreement in Caracas which in effect transforms the wholly-owned Gulf sub-sidiary into a joint enterprise.

An agreement is signed in Toronto between Mene Grande and International Petroleum, a subsidiary of Standard Oil (New Jersey). It was known among the parties as the 'principal agree-ment'; it was announced to the public as a contract of Standard

68

to buy oil from Mene Grande. The principal agreement gave International a supervisory control on all Mene Grande activities, including a veto over major projects. International acquired half of the physical properties of Mene Grande and half of all future production from Mene Grande concessions in Venezuela for $125 million.

Mene Grande and the two subsidiaries of Standard Oil (New Jersey) operating in Venezuela, Lago Petroleum and Standard Oil of Venezuela, sign an agreement in Toronto fixing production quotas for all three companies for the next twelve years. International also participates in the agreement by virtue of the "principal agreement". The "ratio agreement" provided for an output of Standard-Lago 3.454 times that of Mene Grande.

1938

Ramón Díaz Sánchez publishes anti-oil industry novel *"Mene"*.

January
Amid agitated public debate over oil issues and the role of foreign oil companies in the exploitation of Venezuelan oil, the Government announces suspension of the granting of concessions.

March 18
Pres. Lázaro Cárdenas of México signs an Executive Decree expropriating foreign oil properties.

March 20
Exploratory well Tigre-2 (LG-1) of Mene Grande discovers the giant Leona oilfield (Maturín basin, Oficina group, 55 km NE Oficina field).

April 4
Supreme Court orders Mene Grande to pay 16 million bolívars for collecting illegal rebates on some concessions granted during the mid-twenties.

April 15
Second Geological Congress convenes in San Cristóbal.

July 13
After two months of violent debate, the National Congress passes a Hydrocarbons Law (*Ley sobre Hidrocarburos* . . .) containing notable differences to previous laws. The State is authorized to carry on any oil activities. The Law provided for royalties of up to 16% in national reserves, a fortyfold increase of the exploration tax, and a fourfold increase of the initial exploitation tax. Natural gas should be conserved, and a new method of fixing the market value of the oil should be formulated.

September 16
Inauguration of the Geological Institute (Ministry of Education), now the Geology, Mining and Metallurgy School of the Central University of Caracas.

October 13
Standard Oil of Venezuela completes new field wildcat Jusepín-1, discovering one of the largest fields in Venezuela. During 1945, Jusepín produced its 100 millionth barrel of oil (Maturín basin, 35 km w of Maturín).

October 22
Caracas Petroleum, a subsidiary of Ultramar, is incorporated in Caracas.

November 30
Regulations of the 1936 Labour Law are issued.
  International and Nederlandsche Olie Maatschappij, a subsidiary of Shell, sign an agreement in Hudson County, N.J., whereby International sold half of the interests it had acquired the previous year from Mene Grande. The "main agreement", retroactive to December 15, 1937, in fact made NOM(Shell) a full and equal partner with International in the previous arrangements.

International and Shell (through NOM) sign a second document in which Shell recognizes, and assents to the ratio agreement.

December 19
Mene Grande 'reserves its rights' referring to the main agreement between International and NOM.

December 21
The National Congress enacts a new Hydrocarbons Law (*Ley sobre Hidrocarburos y demás minerales combustibles*).

1939

Shell uses palinology (pollen and spores) for the first time in oil exploration. A small laboratory is set up in Maracaibo.

New field wildcat Motatán-1, at the time the deepest well in the country, is suspended by Creole. Total depth is 10,302 feet (Maracaibo basin, 45 km NW of Trujillo, 30 km SE of Mene Grande field).

January 28
In two separate documents, Mene Grande recognizes the right of International to admit NOM(Shell) to the arrangement signed concerning the production and sharing of Venezuelan crude.

February 13
Lagunillas de Agua is completely destroyed a second time by oil blaze in lake. Some reports refer to 3,000 dead.

March 21
Algarrobo-1 is completed as a producer by Varco. This one-well field is now abandoned (Maturín basin, Oficina group, 7 km SW of Yopales field).

April 4
Creole discovers the giant San Joaquín oilfield on completion of

new field wildcat JMN-1 (Maturín basin, Anaco group, 150 km SE of Maturín).

April 5
The Supreme Court rules that Mene Grande should pay 15.5 million bolívars, one fourth of the exploitation tax exempted in 1923.

May 10
Wildcat RPN-1 of Pantepec (now Phillips) discovers the El Roble field of the San Joaquín area (Maturín basin, Anaco group, 12 km NE of San Joaquín field).

June 13
Mene Grande completes Oficina well OG-24, the first dual completion in Eastern Venezuela.

September
A 10-inch pipeline is put into service between the Jusepín field and Caripito by Standard Oil of Venezuela.

September 1
Second World War. Adolph Hitler, Führer of Germany, declares war on Poland.

September 8
Venezuelan Central Bank established. It is to control foreign exchange.

October 7
Creole discovers prolific Eocene production in the Bolívar Coastal field on completion of new pool wildcat LL-370, offshore in Lake Maracaibo.

October 22
The First Petroleum Industry Exhibition is inaugurated by Pres. López-Contreras.

November 6
Venezuela and the United States sign a commercial treaty, the Reciprocal Trade Agreement. Tariff on petroleum exports is reduced by half. Venezuela receives approximately 90% of the import quota.

December
First shipment of crude through 16-inch, 155-km long pipeline from Oficina to Puerto La Cruz. At the time, it was the longest pipeline of its size in the world.

December 4
First shipment of petroleum from Puerto La Cruz terminal.

December 18
Pres. López-Contreras opens First Conference of Government Petroleum Inspectors, in Caracas.

December 31
Yearly production reaches the 200 million barrels mark for the first time.
  Nearly 14 million barrels of crude are processed in Venezuelan refineries.

1940

Two dry holes are drilled in the island of Cubagua.

January 1
Exchange rate of oil dollar fixed at Bs. 3.09 by National Office of Exchange (*Oficina Nacional Centralizadora de Cambios*).

January 24
Regulations to the 1938 Hydrocarbons Law are issued (*Reglamento sobre la Ley* . . .). Development Minister Manuel Egaña declares that the Regulations apply to all concessionaires.

January 26
Texas discovers the small Los Caritos oilfield (Maturín basin, 40 km NE of Temblador field).

February 14
Atlantic discovers the small Socororo field (Maturín basin, Oficina group, 15 km w of Yopales field).

March
Oil companies object to Regulations of the 1938 Hydrocarbons Law, in particular, to the need of a government permit in order to drill a location, to begin new construction and to transfer titles of concessions.

April 17
Creole completes El Roble-2 (RNP-2), bottomed at 10,009 feet, then the deepest hole in South America (El Roble field).

Development Minister Egaña rejects objections of oil companies to the Regulations of the 1938 Hydrocarbons Law.

September 12
Socony makes an important discovery on completion of exploratory well Guario-1 (Maturín basin, Anaco area, 15 km NE of San Joaquín).

October 15
Authority for fixing oil dollar exchange rate given to Central Bank.

December 30
The North Oficina field is discovered by Mene Grande on completion of wildcat OG-116X (Maturín basin, Oficina group, 7 km N of Oficina field).

December 31
Cumulative production of oil in Venezuela reaches now 2,000 million barrels.

January 24
Wildcat RG-2 of Mene Grande discovers the giant Santa Rosa oilfield. During 1959, the field produced its 100 millionth barrel (Maturín basin, Anaco group, 25 km NE of San Joaquín).

March 7
Consolidada de Petróleo (Sinclair) opens up the Santa Bárbara area of the Jusepín field.

March 13
The Pueblo Viejo area of the Bolívar Coastal field opens up on completion of VOC's well LS-645.

April 28
Gen. Isaías Medina-Angarita is elected President of the Republic by the National Congress.

May 23
On settlement of claim raised by Development Minister, Néstor Luis Pérez, in 1937, Mene Grande pays Bs. 30 million for incorrect reporting of transportation costs.

The Trico giant oilfield is discovered by Mene Grande on completion of well OG-168 (Maturín basin, Oficina group, 20 km N of Oficina field).

July 23
Exchange rates are fixed at Bs. 3.09 for oil companies, 3.35 for the public, 4.30 for cacao and 4.60 for coffee (for one dollar).

August 15
Creole completes Las Ollas-1 as the discovery well of a small field (Maturín basin, 35 km W of nearest producing field of Anaco group—El Toco).

October 7
Pres. Medina sends an economic delegation to the United States

to ask for special consideration regarding war export restrictions, since smooth operation of the vital and strategic oil industry of Venezuela was of particular importance to the Allied forces. The mission was unsuccessful.

October 19
Texas well Rincón Largo-1 is successfully completed. This area is now the Santa Ana field.

October 31
Price of diesel oil on the domestic market is lowered by resolution of Ministry of Development.

November 25
The Las Mercedes giant oilfield is discovered by Las Mercedes on completion of new field wildcat Mercedes-2. It produced its 100 millionth barrel during 1961 (Maturín basin, western end, 150 km s of Caracas).

December 26
Creole opens up the Mulata area of the Jusepín field on completion of MC-1 (ex MP-1).

1942

February 14
Seven tankers in the Lake Maracaibo-Curaçao and Aruba run are torpedoed by German submarines.

February 26
Venezuela and Great Britain sign an international treaty delineating the submarine areas in the Gulf of Paria, between Venezuela and Trinidad, by means of median lines. This is the first agreement in the world relating to the continental shelf.

March
Development well GU-3 in the Guario field, at the time the deepest well in the country, is completed by Socony at 10,909 feet total depth.

April 7
Development Minister Enrique Aguerrevere completes first draft of new Hydrocarbons Law.

June 2
Mene Grande makes an important discovery on completion of wildcat GG-1. The giant West Guara field produced its 100 millionth barrel during 1951 (Maturín basin, Oficina group, 20 km NE of Oficina field).

June 15
Pres. Medina receives extraordinary powers to secure smooth operation of oil industry.

July 16
Pres. Medina announces that the petroleum legislation is being revised to ensure the State a greater and more just participation in the subsoil riches of the country.

Minister Aguerrevere signs first agreements with oil companies establishing the commercial value of Venezuelan crudes, in comparison with the actual price of similar crudes in East and West Texas.

July 17
Income taxes are introduced. The first Income Tax Law, to become effective on January 1, 1943, is issued. Oil companies are taxed $2\frac{1}{2}\%$ of their net income (cedular tax) plus a progressive tax related to the amount of net earnings.

August 5
The small Quiamare field is discovered by Mene Grande (Maturín basin, 40 km N of Santa Rosa field—Anaco group).

August 14
Articles against the oil policy of Pres. Medina are published in *La Esfera*.

August 25
Socony completes Anaco-1 as a producer. This one-well field is now abandoned (Maturín basin, Anaco group, 15 km NE of El Roble field).

September 7
An important discovery—the East Guara field—is made by Mene Grande on completion of new field wildcat GG-2. This giant oil-field produced its 100 millionth barrel during 1948 (Maturín basin, Oficina group, 30 km NE of Oficina field).

October 27
The giant Oveja (previously, Aventazón) oilfield is discovered by Mene Grande on successful completion of new field wildcat OM-2X (Maturín basin, Oficina group, 20 km s of Oficina field).

November 15
Pres. Medina reaffirms in Maracaibo the stand of the Executive with respect to the forthcoming petroleum legislation; he said the Government intended to obtain a more equitable share from the exploitation of the oil.

November 20
Consolidada (Sinclair) opens up the Muri area of the Jusepín field.

December 31
Production during the year drops 25% as compared with the previous year. Following shelling of the Aruba and Curaçao refineries by German submarines, a convoy system had been set up. However, tankers were transferred to Europe and the Pacific, while in Venezuela, oil companies could not obtain scarce materials to carry out their programmes.

1943

Rómulo Gallegos publishes "*Sobre la misma Tierra*", a novel.

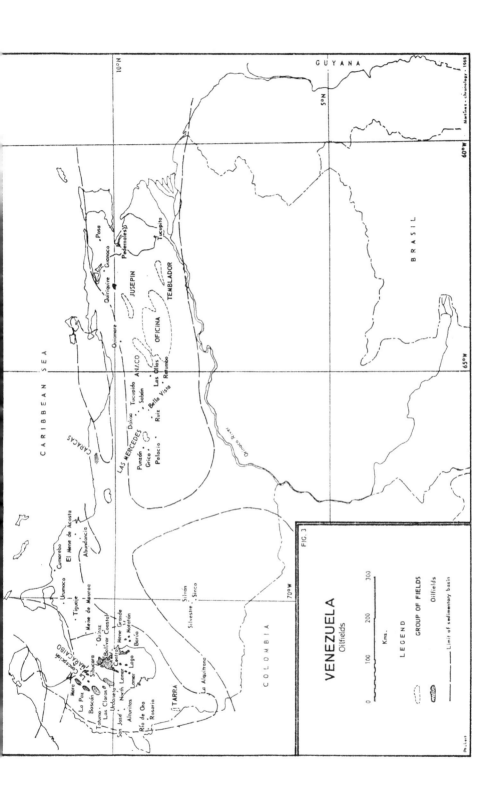

CARIBBEAN SEA

GUYANA

BRASIL

COLOMBIA

VENEZUELA
Oilfields

Kms.
0   100   200   300

LEGEND

GROUP OF FIELDS

Oilfields

Limit of sedimentary basin

FIG. 3

Martinez - chronology - 1988

January 13
Prior to the merging of all interests of Standard Oil (New Jersey) in Venezuela, the Lago Petroleum, Mene Grande, Standard Oil of Venezuela and Nederlandsche Olie Maatschappij execute an agreement cancelling the ratio agreement of December 15, 1937, as of December 31, 1942.

January 30
The United States and Mexico sign an agreement which in effect allows unlimited volumes of Mexican oil to enter the U.S. overland.

February 12
Pres. Proudfit of Standard Oil of Venezuela announces oil companies are in agreement with new petroleum law.

March 5
A congressional commission reports that title to a number of concessions, including that of Valladares and some of Mene Grande in Lake Maracaibo, is contestable.

March 13
National Congress sanctions new Hydrocarbons Law. It was meant to be a mutually profitable arrangement; the Government would receive a greatly enlarged share in the profits (including a minimum of 16 2/3 royalty), in exchange for forty additional years of exploitation, the conversion of all concessions previously granted to the new Law—clearing any claims on the validity or legality of many of them—and the promise of the granting of extensive new areas, for the oil companies. The Law promoted domestic refining and broadened the technical and supervisory powers of the Government. It was published in the Official Gazette Extraordinary 31.

March 16
The General Administration for Income Tax (*Administración General del Impuesto sobre la Renta*) is established.

80

March 21
Organic decree of the Technical Office for Hydrocarbons (*Oficina Técnica de Hidrocarburos*) is issued.

August 19
All interests of Standard Oil (New Jersey) in Venezuela are consolidated in Creole Petroleum Corporation.

August 31
The regulations to the Hydrocarbons Law are issued in Official Gazette Extraordinary 46. The Decree 168 containing the Regulations is dated August 27.

September 15
Mene Grande well YS-2 discovers the Agua Clara (now, the North Yopales) field (Maturín basin, Oficina group, 20 km w of Oficina field).

October 15
The Ostra field is discovered by Mene Grande on completion of wildcat well OM-3X (Maturín basin, Oficina group, 15 km SE of Oficina field).

December 31
Following sanction of the new Hydrocarbons Law, oil companies convert six million hectares to it and give up two million.

Proved reserves of the country are estimated at 5,752 million barrels of oil. From this date on, proved reserves data are published regularly as of year-end.

1944

March 24
The Workers' National Convention (*Convención Nacional de Trabajadores*) is dissolved by decree.

April 21
Pres. Medina starts gigantic concession-granting programme. In less than a year, more acreage is given than that previously held by oil companies. Total area granted was more than $6\frac{1}{2}$ hectares.

April 28
Richmond Exploration, subsidiary of Standard Oil (California), is incorporated in Delaware.

June 20
Socony makes an important discovery in Eastern Venezuela on completion of wildcat Güico-1 (Maturín basin, Oficina group, 5 km w of West Guara field).

July 22
Deeper pool test P-37 in the La Paz oilfield is completed as the discovery well of prolific Cretaceous limestones production. The field is recognized as a giant field; in fact, La Paz is the third largest oilfield in Venezuela, due to the volume of its resources—more than 900 million barrels.

July 27
Income Tax Law is amended.

November 10
Pres. Medina decrees a two-bolívar increase in pay, thwarting the strike of the reorganized labour unions. No social benefits granted.

December
Mene Grande and Creole complete a 16-inch pipeline from the Jusepín group of fields to Puerto La Cruz.

1945

January 28
YS-15 opens up the Moquete area, now integrated into the Yopales field.

March
The Aruba refinery processes its first 1,000 millionth barrel of crude oil, the first in the world to do so.

March 2
Completion of wildcat DM-2 of Caribbean Petroleum, discovering the giant Mara oilfield. The first development areas were designated *Los Tetones* and *Kilómetro 24*. Mara produced its 100 millionth barrel of oil during 1951 (Maracaibo basin, 35 km NW of Maracaibo, 20 km NE of La Paz field).

March 21
GM-2X is completed by Mene Grande as a new field discovery well (Maturín basin, Oficina group, 10 km s of West Guara).

March 30
Avipa-1 is completed as a small producer by Atlantic (Maturín basin, 8 km w of nearest production in Jusepín field).

May 14
New field wildcat Texas-1 of Texas discovers the Tucupita oilfield (Maturín basin, 80 km E of Temblador field).

June 14
An agreement is signed in the Labour Inspector's office in Maracaibo between representatives of oil workers and the operating companies whereby certain minimum conditions are obtained by the unions.

June 21
Creole completes Capacho-1 as an oil producer. Four step out wells are dry (Maturín basin, 5 km w of Tacat field).

September
R-801 of VOC, at the time the deepest well in the country, is suspended by Shell at 13,033 feet (Bolívar Coastal field, La Rosa area).

September 26
The concessions-granting cycle which followed the passing of the 1943 Hydrocarbons Law, is closed.

October 18
Pres. Medina is overthrown. Rómulo Betancourt heads Revolutionary Junta.

December 8
A second agreement, leading to the first Collective Contract, was signed in Caracas between oil workers and company representatives, whereby certain additional benefits are obtained by the unions.

December 12
By resolution of the National Commission of Consumer Goods (*Comisión Nacional de Abastecimiento*) maximum prices are set for gasoline and kerosene sold on the domestic market. At Bs. 0.10 per litre, gasoline price is the lowest in the world.

December 18
Wildcat NG-1 of Socony discovers the giant Nipa oilfield. The field has already produced its 100 millionth barrel (Maturín basin, Oficina group, 10 km N of West Guara field).

December 31
The Revolutionary Junta decrees an extraordinary tax of Bs. 89 million on company earnings.

1946

January
Water injection for pressure maintenance is started in the Oficina field.

January 14
Mene Grande discovers the Caico Seco field on completion of well Caico Seco-1, renamed CaM-1X (Maturín basin, Oficina group, 35 km NW of Oficina field).

January 24
Pres. Betancourt declares that the 1943 Hydrocarbons Law will be respected.

February 19
Mene Grande completes GM-4X as a new field discovery well (Maturín basin, Oficina group, 8 km w of West Guara).

February 26
Sinclair completes first well in the Travieso area of the Jusepín field.

February 27
Grico-1 is completed as a small oil producer by Las Mercedes. Two gas wells and seventeen dry holes were later completed in the area (Maturín basin, 40 km w of Las Mercedes field).

March 7
Socony discovers the West Güico field on completion of wildcat WGV-32 (Maturín basin, Oficina group, 5 km w of Güico field).

March 30
One of the most powerful federations in the Venezuelan Confederation of Labour, *Fedepetrol* (Petroleum Workers Federation) is established at an oil workers congress in Caracas.

April 1
The La Ceiba field is discovered by Mene Grande on completion of well La Ceiba-1, renamed CG-1X (Maturín basin, 25 km NE of Anaco group—Santa Rosa field).

May 17
The South Güico field is discovered by Socony on completion of well SGV-39 (Maturín basin, Oficina group, 10 km s of Güico field).

June 14
The First Collective Contract is signed. The unions obtain payment for the day of rest and fifteen days' paid annual leave.

September 17
Oligocene production is discovered in the Quiriquire field, on completion of deepening work-over Q-216.

September 23
Richmond discovers the Ensenada condensate field on completion of wildcat Zulia 1K-1 (Maracaibo basin, 35 km s of Maracaibo).

October 2
Phillips discovers the Mata Grande oilfield on completion of well FT-1 (Maturín basin, Jusepín group, 10 km w of Santa Bárbara area of Jusepín field).

October 17
The Boscán field, one of the largest accumulations of oil in Venezuela, is discovered by Richmond on completion of new field wildcat Zulia 7F-1. It produced its 100 millionth barrel during 1956 (Maracaibo basin, 50 km sw of Maracaibo).

November 26
Mercedes-33 is completed by Las Mercedes as the discovery well of the Palacio field (Maturín basin, 25 km ssw of Las Mercedes field).

December 19
Richmond discovers the small Macoa oilfield, on completion of new field wildcat Zulia 26D-1 (Maracaibo basin, 110 km sw of Maracaibo).

December 27
The Tucupido field is discovered by Atlantic (Maturín basin, 60 km NE of Las Mercedes field).

December 30
Income Tax Law is amended.

December 31
Daily production average for the year exceeds one million barrels of oil for the first time.

1947

January 23
The small Pelayo field is discovered by Atlantic (Maturín basin, Oficina group, 35 km E of East Guara field).

February 21
Venezuela ratifies the Bretton Woods agreement and becomes member of the International Monetary Fund.

March
Zulia 7G-1, at the time the deepest well in the country, is completed by Richmond at total depth 13,978 feet (Boscán field).

March 18
Mene Grande completes the first electrostatic dehydration installations at Lagunillas.

April 7
New field wildcat GXB-6 of Creole discovers the Lechozo gasfield (Maturín basin, 25 km NW of Las Mercedes).

June 12
Important Cretaceous production is discovered by Colón Development, the West Tarra field, on completion of wildcat WT-2 (Maracaibo basin, Tarra group, 15 km SW of Las Cruces field).

June
A condensate recovery plant goes on stream in the Cumarebo field.

June 26
Minister Pérez Alfonzo announces that one-fourth of the 1948-49

87

royalties, some 36 million barrels of oil, would be marketed directly by the Government.

August
A crude stabilization and treating plant, and gas injection for pressure maintenance, are started in Jusepín.

September 26
The Valle 13 gasfield is discovered by Las Mercedes (Maturín basin, 45 km SE of Las Mercedes field).

October 6
The first of five bids to sell the royalty oil offered by the Government is signed.

October 17
Las Mercedes discovers the small Punzón field (Maturín basin, 30 km W of Las Mercedes field).

December 16
Atlantic discovers the Sabán field on completion of wildcat Sabán 2-1A (Maturín basin, 65 km E of Las Mercedes field).

December 31
Number of oil-producing wells in the country for the first time exceed 5,000.

   Domestic demand (including crude oil used as fuel) exceeds 10 million barrels for the first time.

1948

January 17
Socony discovers the giant Chimire field on completion of new field wildcat Chimire-2, renamed CHV-2 (Maturín basin, Oficina group, 15 km N of Oficina field).

January 22
Creole agrees to pay $0.24 per barrel, instead of $0.19, for the remainder of its royalty oil.

February 1
Socony makes the first discovery in the Barinas basin on completion of new field wildcat San Silvestre-2. The field is later recognized as a giant (35 km SE of Barinas).

February 13
A two-year barter deal, involving 2 million barrels of Venezuelan oil and 5,000 tons of frozen beef from Argentina, is signed.

February 15
Don Rómulo Gallegos is inaugurated President of the Republic.

February 20
Second Collective contract signed. Wages were increased, commissary prices were frozen at cost, three weeks' paid annual leave was granted, housing and many other social benefits were also increased.

February 22
Mene Grande discovers the El Toco oilfield on completion of new field wildcat Toco-1, renamed TM-1 (Maturín basin, Anaco group, 20 km w of Santa Ana field).

March 11
Former Development Minister, Egaña, E. J. Aguerrevere and Deputy Alberto Carnevali are nominated to study the convenience and possibility of building a National Refinery and of exploiting national reserves adjacent to existing fields.

April 29
Collective contract for marine officers signed.

May 4
Collective contract with "marinos" signed.

June
First Cretaceous production in the La Concepción field.

Las Mercedes completes a 16-inch, 250-km pipeline from the Las Mercedes field to Pamatacual.

June 16
Richmond discovers the San José field on completion of new field wildcat Zulia 36E-1 (Maracaibo basin, 110 km sw of Maracaibo).

July
New field wildcat CC-2A in the Curazaíto area, at the time the deepest well in the country, is suspended by Shell at 15,106 feet (8 km N of Tía Juana area of Bolívar Coastal field).

First graduating class of the Petroleum Engineering School of the Caracas Central University.

July 1
The Technical Commission of Mines and Geology assumes the name Institute of Mines and Geology (*Instituto de Minería y Geología*).

July 9
The small Guavinita oilfield is discovered by Las Mercedes (Maturín basin, 30 km sw of Las Mercedes field).

August 11
The small Inca field is discovered by Mene Grande (Maturín basin, Oficina group, 7 km sw of Caico Seco field).

September 8
The Venezuelan Association for Geology, Mining and Petroleum (*Asociación Venezolana de Geología, Minería y Petróleo*) is founded in Caracas.

September 12
The Ganso field is discovered by Mene Grande on completion of

well MFS-1, renamed MS-601X (Maturín basin, Oficina group, 10 km s of East Guara).

Atlantic discovers the Placer gasfield (Maturín basin, 50 km NE of Las Mercedes field).

September 21
Pressure maintenance by gas injection started in Las Mercedes.

October 6
Creole discovers the small Aragua field on completion of wildcat JX-6 (the area is now incorporated into the San Roque field).

October 14
Congress approves report of Permanent Commission for Development referring to Minister's Memoir on the oil industry, specifically, the no-concession policy, the establishment of a national oil company and the possibility of direct sale of royalties.

November 12
National Congress passes a new Income Tax Law, creating the "50-50" sharing of profits. Article 31 establishes an additional tax for the extractive industries of 50 per cent, applicable when oil companies' income, after payment of taxes, exceed the Government's total revenue.

November 24
Pres. Gallegos is ousted; Lt. Col. Carlos Delgado-Chalbaud heads Military Junta.

December 10
Shell discovers the Sibucara field on completion of well S-5. Portions of the proved area of the field are within the city limits of Maracaibo. At the time it was one of the deepest producing fields in the world.

December 14
Creole completes 230-km. pipeline from Ulé, on the eastern shore of Lake Maracaibo, to Amuay, in the Paraguaná peninsula.

December 31
Area under concessions exceeds seven million hectares.

1949

The small Abundancia field is discovered (Falcón basin, 120 km SE of Coro, 25 km SW of El Mene de Acosta field).

January 19
A People's Liberation Committee declares a general strike of petroleum workers throughout Monagas State.

February 1
Wildcat B-1 of Phillips discovers the San Roque field (Maturín basin, Anaco group, 15 km W of San Joaquín field).

The Cardón refinery of Shell starts operations. This, and four other refineries in the country, were built to comply with provisions of the 1943 Hydrocarbons Law.

February 9
Decree 40 establishes the National Commission for Mining and Oil Policies (*Comité Nacional de Política Minera y Petrolera*).

Labour policy of Military Junta is to end political influences out of the worker's unions.

February 23
Secretary General of Fedepetrol, Luis Tovar, in a letter to the Military Junta, requests that all union officials imprisoned since November be liberated.

February 25
A general strike for an indefinite period is ordered by the Venezuelan Confederation of Labour. Decree 56 of the Military Junta dissolves the Confederation and orders new elections for all trade unions, associations and leagues belonging to it.

March 24
Socony discovers the small Silván oilfield on completion of wild-cat Silván-1 (Barinas basin, 10 km NW of Silvestre field).

April 6
The small Tamán oilfield is discovered by Atlantic (Maturín basin, 60 km NE of Las Mercedes field).

April 7
The Military Junta invites the International Labour Office to investigate the freedom of association and the conditions of work in Venezuela.

April 25
Regulations to the Income Tax Laws are issued.

June
J. E. Pogue, then Vice President of the Chase Manhattan National Bank, refers in a paper to the advantages of oil from the Middle East compared with that of Venezuela. As a solution he suggested that the tax arrangements of 1948 be eliminated, that new concessions be granted to the international majors, that no attempt be made to increase the volume of oil refined in the country, and that no further social or economic benefits be granted to the petroleum workers.

June 9
The Ruiz field is discovered by Atlantic and Pancoastal on completion of wildcat Ruiz 3-1 (Maturín basin, 45 km SE of Las Mercedes field).

July 10
Mene Grande discovers the important Mapiri oilfield on completion of wildcat well SG-1 (Maturín basin, Oficina group, 25 km N of Chimire field).

July 12
The small Piragua field is discovered by Las Mercedes (Maturín basin, 40 km sw of Las Mercedes field).

July 29
Well SM-200X of Mene Grande is successfully completed as the discovery well of the Soto giant oilfield, which produced its 100 millionth barrel during 1961 (Maturín basin, Oficina group, 20 km N of Chimire field).

August 23
The Freites field is discovered by Creole on completion of well FX-1 (Maturín basin, Oficina area, 15 km N of Chimire).

August 30
A mission of the International Labour Office concludes its visit to Venezuela, after studying working conditions and freedom of association in the country.

September
Colón Development abandons new field wildcat Río Catatumbo-1 (CT-1), than the deepest hole in Venezuela, at a total depth of 15,637 feet (150 km s of Maracaibo, 10 km from mouth of Catatumbo River).

Minister of Foreign Affairs, L. E. Gómez-Ruiz, and Development Minister, Egaña, appoint Edmundo Luongo Cabello, Luis Emilio Monsanto and Ezequiel Monsalve Casado to a Special Mission for the purpose of paying an official visit to Saudi Arabia, Iran, Egypt, Iraq, Kuwait and Syria. This is the first direct contact between Venezuela and the oil producing countries of the Middle East.

October 1
The agreements concluded by the Ministry of Development and concessionaire companies on the determination of the market value of Venezuelan crude are terminated (except Creole: October 31, 1949).

November 30
The small Pradera oilfield is discovered by Socony (Maturín basin, Oficina group, 20 km NW of Oficina field).

December 2
The United States Federal Trade Commission orders an investigation of the international cartel activities in the oil industry.

December 31
Cumulative production of oil reaches 5,000 million barrels.

1950

First tectonic map of Venezuela published.

January 4
The Amuay refinery of Creole goes on stream.

March 7
The Belén gasfield is discovered by Las Mercedes (Maturín basin, 15 km S of Las Mercedes field).

April 9
Atlantic discovers the Oritupano giant oilfield on successful completion of new field wildcat Oritú-1 (Maturín basin, Oficina group, 40 km E of Leona field).

May
The Puerto La Cruz refinery goes on stream.

May 13
Cosutrapet, the small Communist federation of unions, is dissolved by decree, following an attempt to organize a general strike.

May 23
New field wildcat Los Mangos 1 of Mene Grande discovers a small field (Maturín basin, Oficina group, 15 km NW of Caico Seco field).

May 31
A significant discovery at Dación is made by Mene Grande. This giant field produced its first 100 millionth barrel during 1961 (Maturín basin, Oficina group, 20 km E of East Guara field).

June 25
Korean War starts.

June 30
The International Labour Office publishes its report on the conditions of work and freedom of association in Venezuela. The Military Junta sharply attacks the contents and conclusions of the report.

July 18
New field wildcat Tagua-1 is completed by Mene Grande as a small producer (Maturín basin, Oficina group, 10 km N of Caico Seco field).

July 24
New field wildcat La Vieja-1 is successfully completed by Mene Grande (Maturín basin, 35 km NE of Santa Rosa field).

August
A 130-km water line from Siburúa springs to the refineries in the Paraguaná peninsula is completed by the Government, Creole and Shell.

October 12
The Güere oilfield is discovered by Sinclair on completion of wildcat Güere-1 (Maturín basin, Oficina group, 40 km NW of Chimire field).

October 15
Creole discovers the Alturitas field, on successful completion of Alturitas-1. At a total depth of 17,087 feet, this well was the deepest hole drilled outside the United States at that time (Maracaibo basin, 140 km sw of Maracaibo).

October 21
The El Chaure refinery at Puerto La Cruz goes on stream.

November 13
Col. Delgado-Chalbaud is assassinated. G. Suárez-Flamerich heads Government Junta.

November 14
Gas well Barbacoas-1 is completed by Atlantic (Maturín basin, 30 km N of Las Mercedes field).

November 29
First public posting of oil prices, by Socony in the Middle East.

December 3
Resolution 3825 of the Ministry of Development declares that unitization is compulsory for any reservoir being exploited by two or more operating companies.

December 29
By Royal Decree, the "50-50" principle of profit-sharing is introduced in Saudi Arabia. It is the first country to follow the pattern established by Venezuela in the Income Tax Law of 1948.

December 30
Decree 41 creates the Ministry of Mines and Hydrocarbons.

1951

February 8
Atlantic completes Lechozo-2.

February 15
Mene Grande discovers the Cerro Pelado field on completion of Cerro Pelado-1A, renamed CPZ-1X (Maturín basin, 30 km NE of Anaco group—Santa Rosa field).

March 15
The Iranian Majlis agree to the nationalization of Anglo-Iranian.

March 25
The giant Boca oilfield is discovered by Mene Grande on completion of new field wildcat SG-101X (Maturín basin, Oficina group, 10 km N of Chimire field).

April 1
Monal-1 is completed by Atlantic as an oil producer (Maturín basin, 45 km E of Las Mercedes field).

April 9
The Military Junta issues Decree 114 establishing the temporary norms to regulate the working conditions in the oil industry, in substitution of the collective contract—negotiated by the unions —which had expired.

April 18
Atlantic discovers the Cocomón gasfield, on completion of new field wildcat Copa-1 (TUX-9) (Maturín basin, 75 km E of Las Mercedes field).

April 20
Laloma-2 is completed by Phillips as a small producer (Maturín basin, 5 km E of Anaco group—San Roque field).

May 27
The East Soto field is discovered by Mene Grande on completion of new field wildcat SXM-201 (Maturín basin, Oficina group, 5 km E of Soto field).

May 28

A small field is discovered by Shell on completion of Quiróz-1, renamed QZ-1 (Maracaibo basin, 40 km E of Ambrosió area of Bolívar Coastal field, 25 km S of El Mene de Mauroa field).

DG-1X (Chaparro-1) is completed by Mene Grande as a new field discovery well (Maturín basin, 15 km W of Anaco group—El Toco field).

June 8

GG-301X (North San Tomé-1) is completed by Mene Grande as the discovery well of the Central Guara field (Maturín basin, Oficina group, 20 km NE of Oficina field).

June 28

New formulas to determine the value of Venezuelan crudes, for royalty payment purposes, are established.

July

The School of Petroleum Engineering of the Caracas Central University closes temporarily.

July 2

CaM-301X is completed by Mene Grande as the discovery well of the Tascabaña field (Maturín basin, Oficina group, 10 km W of Chimire field).

July 21

GG-401X is completed by Mene Grande as a new field discovery well (Maturín basin, Oficina group, 8 km E of West Guara field).

July 30

After 712 days total rig time, British Controlled Oilfields abandons new pool wildcat EM-285 at 13,936 feet total depth (El Mene de Mauroa field).

August 10

Apamate-1 (TM-101X) is completed by Mene Grande as a small

producer (Maturín basin, 5 km w of Anaco group—El Toco field).

September 3
Esquina-1R is successfully completed by Socony (Maturín basin, Oficina group, 10 km sw of Chimire field).

September 4
CaZ-401X is completed by Mene Grande as the discovery well of the East Caico field (Maturín basin, Oficina group, 10 km NE of Caico Seco field).

September 18
The First National Petroleum Convention ends.

September 22
Mata-2 is completed by Texas as a new field discovery well (Maturín basin 30 km NE of West Guara field).

October 5
The Organic Statute of Compulsory Social Security Law and its general regulations are enacted.

October 20
Texas discovers the small Mata-1 field (Maturín basin, Oficina group, 20 km N of West Guara).

November 16
Collective Contract with marine officers is signed.

November 23
Collective Contract with marine workers is signed.

December 15
A small discovery is made by Mene Grande on completion of new field wildcat 1-MXZ-1 (Maracaibo basin, 25 km N of La Paz field).

December 24
Shell abandons Conquistado-1 (CQ-1), a new field wildcat spudded in on September 8, 1949. Rig time was 838 days (20 km w of Trujillo).

December 25
New field wildcat Dakoa 8-1 is completed as the discovery well of the Dakoa field by Las Mercedes (Maturín basin, 40 km E of Las Mercedes field).

December 31
A total of 171 crew-months are completed by geological surface parties.

Number of oil wells completed during any one year rise sharply and exceed 1,000 for the first time.

More than 100 million barrels of crude are processed for the first time in Venezuelan refineries.

1952

January 12
Creole successfully completes exploratory well Tapuco-1 (renamed SCJ-1X). Area is now incorporated into the Freites field.

Retumbo-1 is completed by Atlantic as a new field discovery well (Maturín basin, 130 km SE of Las Mercedes field, 110 km E of Oficina field).

January 16
An Executive Commission is established to co-ordinate work in connection with deepening of the Maracaibo Bar.

February 26
Shell completes the "light line", a 30-inch, 255-km pipeline from Palmarejo de Mara to Paraguaná.

April 24
Creole completes Rita-1. This area is now incorporated into the Nardos field.

May

Atlantic completes the gaslines from the Placer, Lechozo, Punzón and Las Mercedes fields to the Caracas and Valencia industrial areas.

May 4

Creole completes new field wildcat Guanoco-2 as a discovery (East Guanoco field). After testing, well was indefinitely suspended later on in the year (Maturín basin, 20 km ESE of Guanoco field).

May 7

Texas discovers the Mata-5 field (Maturín basin, Oficina group, 20 km NE of West Guara field).

May 23

The small Cantaura field is discovered by Socony (Maturín basin, 10 km N of Oficina group—Mapiri field).

May 27

Mene Grande successfully completes new field wildcat CaZ-501X (Maturín basin, Oficina group, 10 km NW of Caico Seco field).

June 21

The Oscurote field is discovered by Socony on completion of well OV-1 (Maturín basin, Oficina group, 25 km NE of West Guara field).

June 27

C-151 is completed by Shell as a deeper pool discovery well in Cretaceous limestone (La Concepción field).

June 29

Phillips completes new field wildcat GC-1, discovering the Bella Vista oilfield (Maturín basin, 55 km SE of Las Mercedes field).

June 30
Autonomous institute of the Ministry of Mines and Hydro-carbons to co-ordinate work of dredging Maracaibo Bar (*Instituto Nacional de Canalizaciones*), is established.

July 9
Wildcat Rincón 5-1 is successfully completed by Texas (Maturín basin, Anaco group, 7 km E of Santa Ana field).

July 24
First postings of Venezuelan crudes. Creole publishes the prices at which it would sell Venezuelan oil in cargo lots at the deep water loading terminals.

July 28
Mercedes completes wildcat Punzón-7 as a small gas producer (Maturín basin, 30 km W of Las Mercedes field).

August 28
A revised trade agreement between Venezuela and the United States is signed in Caracas. There will be no more quotas for petroleum crude of 25° API gravity or more, and products, exported to the U.S., and the tariffs on hydrocarbons are reduced again in half for crudes of less than 25° API gravity.

September
The gasline from the San Joaquín group of fields to Puerto La Cruz is inaugurated.

The general conservation policy for hydrocarbons is presented for the first time at a meeting of the Inter State Oil Compact Commission in Banff, Canada.

September 5
Well ESV-1 of Socony discovers the small East Mapiri field (Maturín basin, Oficina group, 5 km E of Mapiri field).

103

September 12
New field wildcat Mata 3-1 is successfully completed by Texas (Maturín basin, Oficina group, 25 km NE of West Guara field).

OM-501X, formerly South Esquina-1, is completed by Mene Grande as a successful new field wildcat (Maturín basin, Oficina group, 10 km NW of Oficina field).

October 5
An important discovery is made by Creole in the Bolívar Coastal field, on completion of new pool wildcat TJ-319.

October 12
The revised trade agreement between Venezuela and the United States becomes effective. The quota system for petroleum imports into the U.S. is abolished. Tariff on fuel oil is reduced 50 per cent.

October 28
TaG-5A is completed by Mene Grande as the discovery well of the Tácata field. Of nine wells drilled later in the area, one was completed as a gas producer (Maturín basin, 8 km w of Jusepín—Tacat field).

November 12
Mene Grande, a wholly-owned subsidiary of Transocean Gulf—a subsidiary of Gulf, is rechartered in Delaware.

November 15
Wildcat CaZ-201X is completed by Mene Grande as the discovery well of the Caracoles field (Maturín basin, Oficina group, 5 km s of Caico Seco field).

November 19
Roblote-1 is completed by Sinclair as a gas producer (Maturín basin, 25 km w of Anaco group—El Toco field).

November 22
A small field is discovered by Socony on completion of North

Cachama-1, renamed NCV-1R (Maturín basin, Oficina group, 7 km NW of Chimire field).

November 28
LG-501X, formerly Lobo-1, is completed by Mene Grande as a successful new field wildcat (Maturín basin, Oficina group, 30 km E of East Guara field).

November 29
A permanent Inter-ministerial Commission of the Ministries of Finance and Mines and Hydrocarbons is established to study problems relating to the application of the Income Tax Law to the petroleum industry.

December 1
American interests purchase British Controlled Oilfields, one of the oldest operating companies in Venezuela. The syndicate operates under the name Talón Petroleum.

Wildcat Lejos-1 is completed by Mene Grande as a gas producer (Maturín basin, Oficina group, 25 km E of East Guara field).

December 2
Col. Marcos Pérez-Jiménez assumes dictatorial power.

December 5
The Motatán field is discovered by Creole on successful completion of new field wildcat Motatán-2 (Maracaibo basin, 10 km SE of Mene Grande field).

December 22
Wildcat Sapo-1 is completed by Mene Grande as a gas producer (Maturín basin, Oficina group, 3 km SE of Mapiri field).

December 31
Mene Grande (incorporated in Delaware) acquires all assets and business of Mene Grande (a company incorporated in Venezuela).

January 13
The North Chimire field is discovered by Socony on completion of North Chimire-2, renamed NCHV-2 (Maturín basin, Oficina group, 8 km NE of Chimire field).

February 6
Venezuela becomes an associate member of the Inter State Oil Compact Commission.

February 12
New field wildcat NOV-1 is completed successfully by Socony as the discovery well of the important North Oscurote field (Maturín basin, Oficina group, 5 km N of Oscurote field).

February 23
Wildcat SM-501X (Siglo-1) is completed by Mene Grande as the discovery well of the North Soto field (Maturín basin, Oficina group, 20 km N of Chimire field).

March 11
Rositas-2 is worked over by Atlantic and completed as the discovery well of the Rositas field (Maturín basin, 35 km SE of Las Mercedes field).

March 16
Ministry of Mines and Hydrocarbons sets regulations for pricing and transport of natural gas.

April
Prolific production from Basement igneous and metamorphic rocks is discovered in the La Paz oilfield on deepening of well P-86. The level of production of the reservoir and the volume of the resources make this the largest reservoir ever found in non-sedimentary rocks in the world.

April 15
The Venezuelan Constituent Assembly promulgates a new Constitution.

April 16
Wildcat Mata 4-1 is successfully completed by Texas as a discovery well (Maturín basin, Oficina group, 25 km NE of West Guara field).

April 21
The U.S. Department of Justice terminates grand jury proceedings in the international cartel case and files civil suits.

May 7
Compañía Shell de Venezuela, a wholly-owned subsidiary of Bataafse Petroleum Mij., is incorporated in Toronto.

May 23
New field wildcat YS-401X (Yuca-1) of Mene Grande discovers the South Yopales field (Maturín basin, Oficina group, 20 km S of Oficina field).

May 24
Sinclair makes the second discovery in the Barinas basin on completion of new field wildcat Sinco-1. This giant oilfield is the largest so far in the basin, due to the volume of its resources. It produced its 100 millionth barrel during 1965 (5 km s of Silvestre).

May 29
The Tiguaje field is discovered by Texas on completion of new field wildcat Tiguaje-1 (Falcón basin, 130 km SW of Coro).

June 2
The Jobo oilfield is discovered by Creole on completion of wildcat JOM-2, formerly TY-42 (Maturín basin, 25 km SW of Temblador field).

June 8
Mene Grande's MaZ-201X discovers the small Mapuey field (Maturín basin, Oficina group, 10 km w of Caico Secofield).

June 11
New field wildcat LCV-1R is completed successfully by Socony, as the discovery well of the La Ceibita field (Maturín basin, Oficina group, 15 km N of Soto field).

June 15
Tacat-3 is completed by Atlantic as the discovery well of the Tacat field (Maturín basin, Jusepín group, 10 km w of Santa Bárbara area, Jusepín field).

Wildcat Rincón 7-1 is successfully completed by Texas as a discovery well (Maturín basin, Anaco group, 10 km E of Santa Ana field).

August 8
Junta 11-2, formerly designated Junta-2, is completed successfully by Atlantic as a new field discovery well (Maturín basin, Oficina group, 10 km w of Oritupano field).

August 20
New field wildcat NS-601X of Mene Grande discovers the Nigua field (Maturín basin, Oficina group, 10 km N of West Guara field).

September 1
Well ZM-1X of Mene Grande discovers the Zorro field (Maturín basin, Oficina group, 10 km N of Zumo field).

September 2
The Zeta-1 wildcat is completed by Mene Grande as a discovery well (Maturín basin, Oficina group, 30 km N of West Guara field).

September 12
Collective Contract signed with the oil companies by (unrepresen-

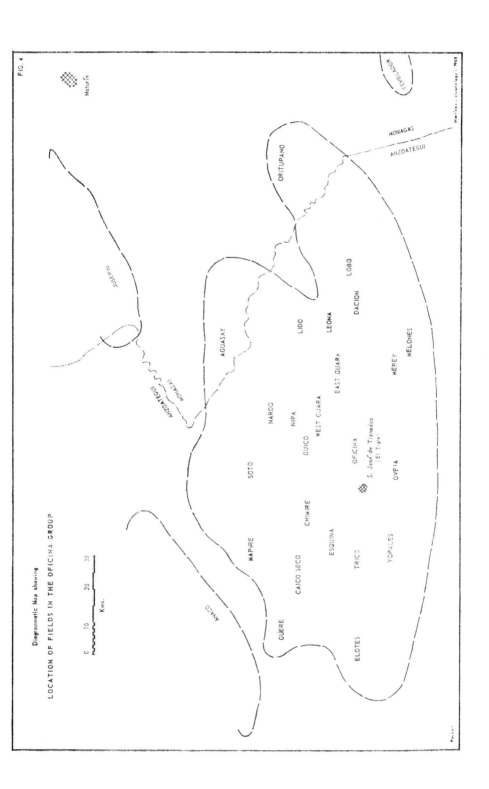

FIG. 4

Diagrammatic Map showing

LOCATION OF FIELDS IN THE OFICINA GROUP

tative) Independent Union Oil Committee (*Comité Petrolero Sindical Independiente*).

September 17
LS-1387, a deeper pool test of Shell in the Lagunillas area of the Bolívar Coastal field, is abandoned dry at a total depth of 17,537 feet, the deepest hole then drilled outside the United States.

September 23
Socony completes Santa Fé-1 as a small oil producer. Two wells drilled later in the area were dry.

October 6
The small Adobe field is discovered by Mene Grande on completion of well Adobe-1, renamed AdM-1X (Maturín basin, Oficina group, 20 km w of Oritupano field).

October 21
The small Casca (Cascaroncito) field is discovered by Mene Grande (Maturín basin, 35 km NW of Anaco group—Santa Ana field).
    The small Kaki field is discovered by Mene Grande (Maturín basin, Oficina group, 8 km w of Mapiri field).

October 24
New field wildcat OX-401X is completed by Mene Grande as the discovery well of the Oca field (Maturín basin, Oficina group, 20 km SE of Oficina field).

October 26
East Pilón-2 is completed by Creole as the discovery well of the Isleño field (Maturín basin, 20 km SE of Temblador field).

November 5
Collective Contract signed by the marine workers and oil companies.

November 14
Shell recompletes DM-22 as the first Basement well of the Mara field.

November 28
Alturitas-2 is suspended by Creole after 542 rig days. At a total depth of 17,265 feet it is the second deepest well in Venezuela.

December 31
Proved reserves of the country exceed 10,000 million barrels of crude petroleum for the first time.

1954

January 22
Mene Grande discovers the Zumo field on completion of wildcat ZM-101X (Maturín basin, Oficina group, 30 km NE of West Guara field).

February 27
Collective Contract with marine officers signed by oil companies.

March 13
Mene Grande completes wildcat IZ-101X as the discovery well of the small Isla field (Maturín basin, Oficina group, 10 km SW of Caico Seco field).

April 5
An important discovery is made by Mene Grande on completion of NZ-701X, formerly Nardo-1 (Maturín basin, Oficina group, 20 km NE of West Guara field).

April 8
New field wildcat Cagigal-1 is completed by Shell as a small producer (Maturín basin, 120 km NE of Las Mercedes field, 80 km W of San Joaquín field).

April 24
The Araibel field is discovered by Socony on successful comple-

tion of wildcat ARV-1R (Maturín basin, Oficina group, 25 km NE of Chimire field).

April 27
Coporo-1 is completed by Creole (Maturín basin, 110 km SE of Las Mercedes field).

June 16
Mene Grande discovers the small Nieblas field (Maturín basin, Oficina group, 15 km NE of West Guara field).

June 24
Mahomal-1 is completed by Sinclair as a new condensate field discovery well (Maturín basin, 90 km ESE of Las Mercedes field).

June 29
New pool wildcat VLA-14 is completed by Shell in the Paleocene Guasare formation (Bolívar Coastal field).

July 19
New field wildcat Elotes-1 (ES-1X) is successfully completed by Mene Grande (Maturín basin, Oficina group, 50 km W of Oficina field).

July 20
Wildcat well LZ-601X of Mene Grande discovers the giant Limón oilfield (Maturín basin, Oficina group, 15 km N of East Guara field).

July 24
BU-4, the fourth of the Burgúa wildcats drilled by Shell is abandoned (Burgúa area: 55 km SE of San Cristóbal, in western-most part of Apure State).

July 28
Wildcat LG-701X of Mene Grande discovers the Lido oilfield (Maturín basin, Oficina group, 15 km NE of East Guara field).

July 31
New field wildcat T-189 is completed by Shell as a non-commercial producer (Tarra group).

September
School of Petroleum Engineering of Zulia University in Maracaibo starts functioning.

September 30
A small field is discovered by Mene Grande on completion of NS-50X, formerly Nidos-1 (Maturín basin, Oficina group, 30 km N of Chimire).

October 9
Mata 8-1 is successfully completed by Texas. No further drilling is undertaken in the field (Maturín basin, Oficina group, 25 km NW of West Guara field).

October 20
Wildcat Dakoa 10-1 is completed by Las Mercedes as an oil producer (Maturín basin, 30 km E of Las Mercedes field).

October 29
An agreement is signed between Iran and a consortium of oil companies, thus ending the situation created by the nationalization of the industry in 1951.

November 9
The small Manresa field is discovered by Creole on completion of new field wildcat MR-1, formerly JX-8 (Maturín basin, 25 km N of Jusepín field).

November 19
The West Nipa field is discovered by Socony on successful completion of new field wildcat W-NV-51R (Maturín basin, Oficina group, 5 km W of Nipa field).

December 31
Casón-1 is successfully completed by Mene Grande (Maturín basin, 30 km NW of Anaco group—El Tocó field).

More than 11 million hectares are explored by aerogeology.

Capacity of Venezuelan refineries exceed 500,000 barrels of crude per day for the first time.

Domestic consumption of petroleum products exceeds 30 million barrels for the first time.

1955

January 11
Friata-1, commenced on December 24, 1952, in northern Táchira State, is abandoned dry by Shell.

February 1
Shell posts the prices of its Venezuelan crudes.

April 7
Mene Grande discovers the small AdM-101 producing area on completion of well AdM-101X (Maturín basin, Oficina group, 5 km W of Oritupano field).

April 10
Creole completes new field wildcat UD-1 (ex TJ-342), the discovery well of the Urdaneta giant oilfield (Maracaibo basin, along western shores of Lake Maracaibo, 60 km S of Maracaibo).

April 19
The Dakoa-16 field is discovered by Las Mercedes on completion of gas well Dakoa 16-3; first oil completion is Dakoa 16-9 (Maturín basin, 43 km E of Las Mercedes field).

April 27
The Valle-17 oilfield is discovered by Las Mercedes (Maturín basin, 45 km SE of Las Mercedes field).

May 11
The Aníbal field is discovered by Atlantic (Maturín basin, 40 km w of nearest Oficina field—Elotes).

May 24
Texas discovers the Mata-9 field (Maturín basin, Oficina group, 20 km NE of West Guara field).

May 25
Wildcat Boca Ricoa-1 is completed by Creole as a small producer (Falcón basin, 15 km NE of Cumarebo field).

June 11
Texas discovers the Mata-12 field (Maturín basin, Oficina group, 25 km NE of West Guara field.

June 20
SOM-3A is completed by Shell as the discovery well of the small South Maracaibo gasfield (Maracaibo basin, 15 km s of Maracaibo).

July 25
The Oleos wildcat (renamed OS-601X) is successfully completed by Mene Grande (Maturín basin, Oficina group, 20 km E of Oveja field).

July 26
Income Tax Law is amended.

August 13
Texas discovers the Mata-11 field (Maturín basin, Oficina group, 20 km N of West Guara field).

August 14
An important discovery is made by Mene Grande in the Oficina area of Eastern Venezuela on completion of wildcat MS-401X, formerly Melones-1 (Maturín basin, Oficina group, 35 km SE of East Guara field).

August 29
Minor amendment to the 1943 Hydrocarbons Law. Drilling of what really are exploratory wells, as if they were shallow holes dug for exploration surveys, is prohibited.

October 27
Sinclair makes a significant discovery on completion of wildcat Aguasay-1 (Maturín basin, Oficina group, 40 km NE of West Guara field).

December 20
The Zapatos giant field is discovered by Mene Grande on completion of wildcat ZM-301X (Maturín basin, Oficina group, 40 km NE of Chimire field).

December 27
Wildcat SM-150X of Mene Grande is completed as the discovery well of the Soyas field (Maturin basin, Oficina group, 15 km N of Chimire field).

December 31
Daily average production from Venezuelan fields exceeds 2 million barrels for the first time.

A record 171 exploratory wells are completed during the year.

1956

The Venezuelan stratigraphic lexicon is published.

January 11
Regulations of the Income Tax Law are issued.

January 12
Ministry of Mines and Hydrocarbons announces that concessions will be granted soon.

March 16
Texas discovers the small Mata-13 field (Maturín basin, Oficina group, 30 km NE of West Guara field).

May 19
The small Juanita field is discovered by Sinclair (Maturín basin, Oficina group, 5 km w of Elotes field).

June 1
Decree 356 sets forth regulations for the use of the deep channel dredged in the Maracaibo Bar.

June 4
AdM-301X, discovery well of the Adas field, is completed by Mene Grande (Maturín basin, Oficina group, 15 km s of Oritupano field).

June 6
The Pato wildcat is successfully completed by Mene Grande. Four other wells drilled later in the area were dry (Maturín basin, 15 km E of Anaco group—Santa Rosa field).

June 7
Texas 14-1 A is completed by Texas as a small oil producer (Maturín basin, Oficina group, 20 km NE of West Guara field).

June 15
Phillips completes Gozo-2 as a gasfield discovery well (Maturín basin, 50 km SE of Las Mercedes field).

June 21
Libro-1 (renamed LG-901X) of Mene Grande discovers a small field (Maturín basin, Oficina group, 10 km E of Lobo field).

June 30
Decree 367 of the Ministry of Mines and Hydrocarbons establishes the Venezuelan Institute of Petrochemicals (*Instituto Venezolano de Petroquímica*).

July 11
Mene Grande discovers the North Zumo field on completion of ZM-201X (Maturín basin, Oficina group, 5 km N of Zumo field).

Adrales-1 (AdM-401X) is completed by Mene Grande as a new field discovery well (Maturín basin, Oficina group, 10 km w of Oritupano field).

July 27
Law relating to the Territorial Sea, Continental Shelf, Protection of Fisheries and Air Space is passed.

August 8
FZ-250X is completed by Mene Grande as the discovery well of the Finca field (Maturín basin, Oficina group, 30 km NW of Oficina field).

August 21
Concession granting cycle starts. Shell, Mene Grande, Superior and Venezuelan American Independent Oil Producers are granted twenty-seven parcels covering 20,000 hectares in Lake Maracaibo.

September 6
LM-50X (Leguas-1) is completed by Mene Grande as an oil producer (Maturín basin, Oficina group, 12 km E of East Guara field).

September 19
LM-250X (Levas-1), of Mene Grande, discovers a small field (Maturín basin, Oficina group, 25 km SE of East Guara field).

October 6
Aguasay-3 is completed by Sinclair as a new field discovery (Maturín basin, Oficina group, 45 km NE of West Guara field).

October 11
Mene Grande completes as an oil producer well LG-550X,

formerly Lustro-1 (Maturín basin, Oficina group, 3 km s of Lobo field).

October 17
LM-301X (Lestes-1) is completed by Mene Grande as an oil producer (Maturín basin, Oficina group, 5 km NE of Lobo field).

October 19
Collective Contract signed between National Confederation of Workers (*Confederación Nacional de Trabajadores de Venezuela*) and operating oil companies.

October 26
Collective Contract with marine workers signed by oil companies.

December 6
Mene Grande receives 22,960 hectares in 47 parcels in Lake Maracaibo. Last concessions granted during the year.

December 25
Icaco-1 is completed as a gas producer by Mene Grande, but no further drilling is done in the area (Maturín basin, Oficina group, 6 km s of Caico Seco field).

December 26
Ministry of Mines and Hydrocarbons fixes for the first time rates for ships using the new channel across Maracaibo Bar. Majority of shipping involves oil tankers.

December 31
Number of oil-producing wells in the country for the first time exceed 10,000.

1957
January 3
Texas discovers the small Mata-14 field (Maturín basin, Oficina group, 25 km NE of West Guara field).

January 21
A resolution of the Ministry of Mines and Hydrocarbons assigns to the Petrochemicals Institute the administration of a national network of gas pipelines.

February 7
Chaparrito 5-1 is completed by Texas as a small producer (Maturín basin, Anaco group, 4 km s of El Tocó field).

February 25
Mercedes completes Valle 3-1 as a new field discovery well (Maturín basin, 40 km SE of Las Mercedes field).

March 3
Socony discovers the small North Nipa field on completion of wildcat NV-101 (Maturín basin, Oficina group, 5 km N of Nipa field).

March 5
La Freitera-1 is completed by Socony as an oil producer. No other wells drilled in the area (Maturín basin, Oficina group, 35 km N of Chimire field).

March 14
One 9,550 hectares concession is granted to Venezuelan American, first during the year.

April–May
Seven private companies conduct an aeromagnetic survey covering most of Apure and Barinas States.

April 22
Mene Grande completes the first producer in the Ceuta area of the Bolívar Coastal field.

May 17
Ira-1 is completed by Mene Grande as an oil producer (Maturín basin, Oficina group, 25 km w of Caico Seco field).

May 20
Well MG-401X (Miga-1) is completed by Mene Grande as a new field discovery well (Maturín basin, Oficina group, 30 km SE of Oficina field).

June 2
Galán-1 is completed as a new field discovery well by Socony. No more drilling done in the area (Maturín basin, 8 km N of Oficina group—Mapiri field).

June 6
Lama-1 of Superior spuds in.

June 26
Creole inaugurates second offshore huge gas reinjection plant TJ-2 in Tía Juana area of Bolívar Coastal field.

July 29
A voluntary programme for control of oil imports into the United States (east of the Rocky Mountains) is established. The U.S. Secretary of Interior appoints a Special Assistant to administer the programme.

August 1
CL-1 is completed by Creole as the discovery well of a giant field (Maracaibo basin, central area of Lake Maracaibo, 100 km S of Maracaibo, 30 km W of Ceuta area of Bolívar Coastal field).

August 23
New field wildcat UD-41 is completed by Creole as the discovery well of a small field (Maracaibo basin, offshore Lake Maracaibo, 45 km S of Maracaibo).

September
First all-aluminium drilling platforms are installed offshore Lake Maracaibo for Superior.

September 7
Superior makes the first discovery in the concessions granted during 1956 and 1957: Lama-1 is completed as a successful new pool wildcat (Bolívar Coastal field).

Creole successfully completes Cachipo-2, renamed PGQ-12 (Maturín basin, 10 km s of Quiriquire field).

September 15
Mene Grande completes well GM-850X (Grúas-1) as the discovery well of the North Guara field (Maturín basin, Oficina area, 6 km N of West Guara field).

October 6
Large reservoirs of Eocene and Cretaceous (Mito Juan formation) age are discovered by Sun on completion of new field discovery well SVSX-1, in its recently granted concession in Lake Maracaibo, south of Superior leases, Lama area (Bolívar Coastal field).

October 16
Superior starts production 14 months following the grant of titles.

October 20
Richmond discovers the Los Claros giant oilfield on completion of wildcat Zulia 22D-1 (Maracaibo basin, 60 km SW of Maracaibo).

October 30
Creole receive 66 exploitation parcels covering 30,667 hectares in Monagas State. This closes concession granting cycle. A total of 510,350 hectares of exploration–exploitation concessions and 310,757 hectares of exploitation concession were granted in 1956 and 1957, at a cost of 685 million dollars. At least one-seventh of the volume of resources of the country were given to the concessionaries.

November 12
After drilling one dry hole in its new concession in Lake Maracaibo,

Signal successfully completes new field wildcat Centro-2X as the discovery well of the Centro oilfield (Maracaibo basin, 80 km s of Maracaibo, 15 km s of nearest production in Bolívar Coastal field).

November 20
New field wildcat Palmita-1 is completed by Socony as a producer. It is the first discovery in the Barinas basin in four years (5 km N of Silvestre field).

December 2
Collective Contract signed by oil companies with marine officers.

December 7
San Jacinto, operator of a group of companies in recently granted concessions, completes Marlago-1 as a new pool discovery (Ceuta area, Bolívar Coastal field).

December 12
U.S. Voluntary Oil Imports Programme is extended to cover also area west of Rocky Mountains.

December 31
More than 1,000 million barrels of oil are produced during a single year for the first time. Cumulative production exceeds now 10,000 million barrels and proved reserves, 15,000 million barrels. A record 1,597 million barrels of crude were discovered during the year.

Seven and one-half million hectares are covered by seismic exploration.

A record 1,739 wells are completed during the year.

January 23
Dictator Pérez-Jimenez is ousted by popular uprising; Rear Adm. W. Larrazábal heads Provisional Government Junta.

January 26
Creole completes El Salto-11 as a small oil producer (Maturín basin, 25 km E of Oficina group—Oritupano field).

February 6
Venezuelan Petroleum becomes Sinclair Venezuelan Oil.

February 12
Mene Grande discovers the Yucal gasfield (Maturín basin, 60 km N of Las Mercedes field).

February 15
U.S. Subsecretary of State for Latin America visits Venezuela regarding changes to introduce in the Imports Programme.

February 20
The Ipire-7 field is discovered by Las Mercedes (Maturín basin, 120 km SE of Las Mercedes field, 120 km W of Oficina group—Oficina field).

March
Shell starts the first large scale steam injection secondary recovery project in the world, in the Cabimas area of the Bolívar Coastal field.

Rosal-1 is completed by Sinclair as the discovery well of a small field (Maturín basin, 10 km N of Anaco group—Santa Rosa field).

Delegation presided by the U.S. Undersecretary of State for Economic Affairs holds discussions in Caracas. The Ambassador of Canada also attends.

March 4
Shell discovers the Barúa oilfield on completion of new field wildcat MGB-1X (Maracaibo basin, 8 km SSW of Mene Grande field).

March 10
Las Mercedes discovers the Ipire-8 field (Maturín basin, 110 km w of Oficina group of fields).

March 28
A small producer is completed by Mene Grande at North Santa Rosa (Maturín basin, Anaco group, 15 km NE of Santa Rosa field).

April 11
A one-well field is discovered by Mene Grande on completion of Cascadas-1, renamed CCM-1X (Maturín basin, 25 km WNW of Anaco group—El Toco field).

April 12
New field wildcat POSA 112-1 is first well successfully completed offshore in the Venezuelan portion of the Gulf of Paria. A total of seven wells were drilled later in the field, which has not been put on production (30 km NE of Pedernales field).

April 27
The small Bucaral field is discovered by Socony (Maturín basin, 10 km SE of San Joaquín field, 10 km NW of Mapiri field).

May 12
The Ipire 2 field is discovered by Las Mercedes (Maturín basin, 120 km SE of Las Mercedes field).

May 20
Report of an investigating commission is submitted to the Government Junta concerning the concession granting programme of 1956-57. All legal procedures were found indisputable.

May 22
New field wildcat 6Y-2X of Mene Grande is completed as the

discovery well of the North Lamar field (Maracaibo basin, offshore in Lake Maracaibo, 12 km NE of Lamar field, 15 km SE of nearest area of Bolívar Coastal field—Lama).

June 4
The United States issues Regulations relating to imports of unfinished oils.

July 1
Transport, storage and installation of systems for handling of liquid petroleum gases can only be carried on with permit from Ministry of Mines and Hydrocarbons.

July 10
Income Tax Law is amended, providing for a general increase in the level of taxation.

July 12
The small Maporal field is discovered by Socony (Barinas basin, 8 km N of Silvestre field).

July 28
Texas discovers the small Mata-17 field (Maturín basin, Oficina group, 25 km NE of West Guara field).

August 8
Mene Grande discovers the Lago field on successful completion of new field wildcat 2Y-2X (Maracaibo basin, offshore in Lake Maracaibo, 100 km S of Maracaibo, 10 km E of Lama area of Bolívar Coastal field).

August 12
The (Finance and Mines and Hydrocarbons) Inter-ministerial Commission is to study also problems relating to refining and transportation in the petroleum industry.

August 25
Texas discovers the small Mata-19 field (Maturín basin, Oficina group, 20 km NE of West Guara field).

September 10
U.S. Oil Import Administration proposes import quotas be given only to domestic refiners (so-called Carson plan).

October 3
The Morichal giant oilfield is discovered by Phillips on completion of new field wildcat MPG-4-1 (Maturín basin, 40 km SW of Temblador field).

Valle 11-1 is completed by Las Mercedes as a small oil producer (Maturín basin, 40 km SE of Las Mercedes field).

November 27
New field wildcat LPG 114-3 of Phillips discovers the Lamar giant field, in new concessions given the previous year offshore in Lake Maracaibo. By year-end 1963, the Lamar oilfield had already produced its first 100 millionth barrel (Maracaibo basin, 110 km s of Maracaibo, 30 km s of Lama area of Bolívar Coastal field).

December 7
Presidential elections. Rómulo Betancourt is elected.

December 13
Socony completes Estero-1 as a small producer (Barinas basin, 3 km N of Silvestre field).

December 17
U.S. Undersecretary of State for Economic Affairs again visits Venezuela for discussion of the discriminatory provisions in the imports programme.

December 19
Decree 476 of Provisional Pres. Edgar Sanabria introduces changes in the Income Tax Law, increasing tax rates to a maximum of 46

per cent of net earnings, in addition to the "cedular" income tax of 1.5 per cent. When combined with royalties and other tax payments, the Venezuelan Government revenue increases to 66-67 per cent of the industry's gross profits.

December 23
Law for practising Engineering and Similar Professions (*Ley del Ejercicio de la Ingeniería y Profesiones afines*) is sanctioned by Provisional President Sanabria.

December 31
Largo-1 is completed by Socony as an oil producer (Maturín basin, 15 km N of Oficina group—Soto field).

1959

January 16
The post of Petroleum Counsellor is established in the Venezuelan Embassy in Canada.

January 17
Sanvi 5-1 is completed by Las Mercedes as a small producer (Maturín basin, Oficina group, 12 km NW of Elotes field).

February 6
Shell starts a general reduction of the posted prices of Venezuelan oils. A week later (February 12th), reductions of even larger amounts are introduced in the Middle East; posted prices in the United States remain unchanged, making the breakdown of the international crude oil pricing structure evident.

President of Creole is replaced. He had sharply criticized in a letter the amendment to the Income Tax Law; Mines and Hydrocarbons Minister, Julio Diez, had flatly rejected the contents of the letter.

March 10
Proclamation 3279 by U.S. Pres. Eisenhower establishes manda-

tory control of oil imports into the United States. Imports are considered to be a threat to national security.

March 11
LG-353X (Lazo-1) is completed as an oil producer by Mene Grande (Maturín basin, Oficina group, 20 km E of Lobo field).

March 26
The small Barso field is discovered by Atlantic on completion of well Barso 12-2 (Maturín basin, 100 km ESE of Las Mercedes field).

April 4
Posted prices of Venezuelan crude oils are uniformly reduced by operating companies.

April 9
The Coordinating Commission for the Conservation and Commerce of Hydrocarbons is created by Resolution 557 of the Ministry of Mines and Hydrocarbons. The Commission shall be "capable of studying and recommending the regulations on the commerce of hydrocarbons and of coordinating them with the conservation policy advised by the supreme interest of the nation."

April 20
Secret consultations take place in Cairo, at the time of the First Arab Petroleum Congress, between the delegates of Venezuela, Iran, United Arab Republic and Kuwait, and the Head of the Petroleum Department of the Arab League. This meeting set up the general agreement on the establishment of an "oil consultation commission" later to be known as OPEC.

May 3
A small oil accumulation is discovered by Las Mercedes on completion of well Dakoa 20-1 (Maturín basin, 40 km E of Las Mercedes field).

May 13
Minister Pérez Alfonzo explains the Venezuelan position with respect to discriminatory provisions in the imports programme to the U.S. Secretaries of Commerce, State and Interior.

May 14
Budare-1 is completed by Socony as an oil producer (Maturín basin, Oficina group, 15 km sw of Elotes field).

May 25
Minister of Foreign Affairs insists in a letter to United States Ambassador that consultations at high levels are necessary to preserve the price of Venezuelan oils on the international markets, in view of the introduction of a programme of crude imports in the U.S.

May 27
Minister Pérez Alfonzo, addressing the Chamber of Deputies of the National Congress, gives a summary of the national petroleum policy.

June 30
Fundación Shell is established.

July 7
Ministry of Mines and Hydrocarbons decree 850 establishes a Commission to plan the formation of petroleum technicians.

July 14
Maulpa-1 is completed by Socony as an oil producer (Maturín basin, 10 km N of Oficina group—Soto field).

July 24
Shell completes CR-2 as the discovery well of the (El) Rosario field (Maracaibo basin, 190 km sw of Maracaibo, 50 km N of Tarra group—Los Manueles field).

August 18
Sun's 100,000 barrels per day automatic flow station on Lake Maracaibo goes on stream.

August 21
Icón-1 (IZ-104X) is completed by Mene Grande as a gas producer (Maturín basin, Oficina group, 15 km sw of Caico Seco field).

August 22
Law establishing National Institute for Educational Cooperation (*Instituto Nacional de Cooperación Educativa—INCE*), to provide a programme of skilled training and apprenticeship.

September 11
The National Energy Council (*Consejo Nacional de Energía*) is established.

September 17
Ida-1 is completed by Mene Grande as a gas producer, but no further drilling is undertaken in the area (Maturín basin, Oficina group, 10 km NW of Elotes field).

October
Establishment of the Venezuelan Embassy in Cairo, with jurisdiction in the U.A.R., Saudi Arabia and Iraq. Dr. Antonio Martín Araujo is appointed first Ambassador.

October 14
Venezuela attends as observer, the 7th meeting of the Committee of Arab Petroleum Experts in Jeddah (Saudi Arabia). Dr. Eduardo Acosta, the Venezuelan representative, stated unequivocally that "only with the cooperation of the Middle East exporting countries" could oil prices be maintained.

November 29
The IIIrd Venezuelan Geological Congress ends in Caracas.

December
Treasury borrows Bs. 300 million from a group of United States commercial banks, against future tax collections. Loan repaid in March and May.

Sinclair discovers the East Aguasay field on completion of new field wildcat E. Aguasay-2 (Maturín basin, Oficina group, 20 km E of Aguasay field).

December 3
Ministry of Mines and Hydrocarbons (*Oficio circular* 3825) makes compulsory unitization of reservoirs exploited by more than one concessionaire.

1960

The Venezuelan College of Engineers establishes an Office of Control for Authorizations, to issue permits to foreign graduates (mostly geologists and petroleum engineers), as per provisions of the 1958 Law for practising the engineering profession.

February 13
Fedepetrol and oil companies sign new Collective Contract.

February 19
The Jobal new field wildcat of Socony is completed as a small oil producer (Maturín basin, 70 km NE of Las Mercedes field).

February 28
IM-601-X (Iris-1) is completed by Mene Grande as an oil producer (Maturín basin, 20 km SW of Oficina group—Güere field).

March 17
Unitization agreement for Lower Lagunillas reservoir signed by Shell, Creole, Mene Grande and San Jacinto (Bolívar Coastal field).

April 5
Collective Contract signed by oil companies with marine workers union.

April 19
The Venezuelan State oil company, *Corporación Venezolana del Petróleo*—CVP—is established by decree 260 of Pres. Betancourt, published in the Official Gazette No. 26,234 of April 22.

April 20
Paria Operations discovers second offshore oilfield in the Venezuelan portion of the Gulf of Paria, on completion of new field wildcat POSA 117-1. One step-out well was later successfully completed, but the field has not been developed further (Maturín basin, 25 km NE of Pedernales field).

May 3
In a speech in Dallas at the annual TIPRO meeting, Min. Pérez Alfonzo reaffirms Venezuelan views on oil production programming, exports and prices.

August 9
Resolution 994 of the Ministry of Mines and Hydrocarbons informs concessionaires that production of oil to be sold at what the Coordinating Commission considers "abnormal discounts", will not be permitted.

Esso reduces, by as much as $0.14 per barrel, the postings of its crudes in the Persian Gulf.

August 12
Minister of Petroleum Affairs of Saudi Arabia, Tariki, and Director General of the Arab League Petroleum Department, Salman, approach Minister Pérez Alfonzo, concerning the reductions of postings in the prices of Middle East oil.

In accordance with Resolution 994, production of some companies is ordered closed.

August 15
Shell also reduces posted prices in the Persian Gulf (crudes from Iraq and Qatar), following Esso reductions.

August 16
British Petroleum brings down posted prices of its crudes by no more than $0.10 per barrel.

August 20
Creole successfully completes wildcat Acema-1 (Maturín basin, Oficina group, 20 km E of Aguasay field).

September 3
The Government of Iraq invites delegations at the highest level from Iran, Kuwait, Saudi Arabia and Venezuela, to meet in one week in Baghdad, in connection with the reductions in posted prices of Middle East oils started August 9th.

September 10
Socony announces a reduction in the posted prices of its Persian Gulf crudes to BP-indicated levels.

A meeting of representatives of Iran, Kuwait, Saudi Arabia and Venezuela convenes in Baghdad.

September 14
Esso announces an increase of $0.04 per barrel for its Persian Gulf crudes.

OPEC—the Organization of Petroleum Exporting Countries —is established, following a four-day meeting in Baghdad between Iran, Iraq, Kuwait, Saudi Arabia and Venezuela. The principal aim of the Organization shall be "the unification of petroleum policies among Member Countries and the determination of the best means for safeguarding the interests of Member Countries individually and collectively" (para. 4 of Resolution I.2). Dr. Pérez Alfonzo represented Venezuela.

September 24
Publication in Caracas, Baghdad, Riyadh, Kuwait and Tehran of the treaty establishing OPEC.

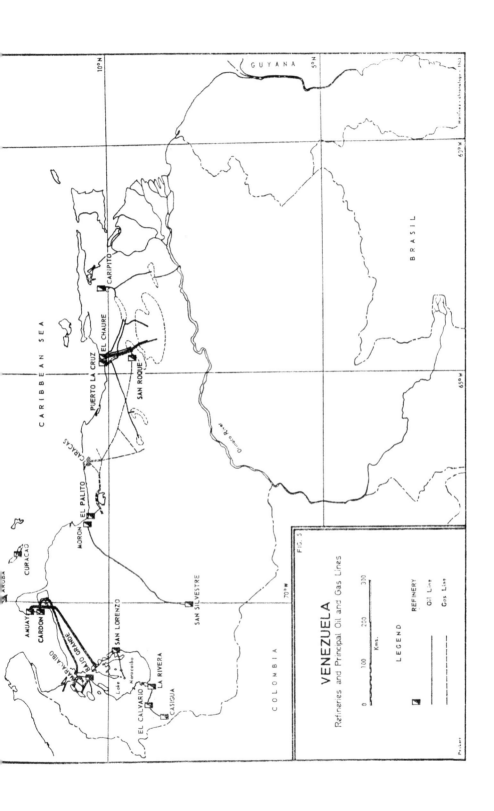

VENEZUELA

Refineries and Principal Oil and Gas Lines

LEGEND

REFINERY

Oil Line

Gas Line

0 100 200 300
Kms.

FIG. 5

October 22
A strong Venezuelan delegation attends the 2nd Arab Petroleum Congress in Beirut.

December 4
A sub-committee meets in Baghdad to discuss the budget, statutes and headquarters of OPEC.

December 27
First directorate of the CVP is named.

December 31
Volume of estimated proved reserves stand at 17,404 million barrels, an all-time high.

Wells completed during the year drop to 444.

Capacity of Venezuelan refineries exceeds one million barrels of crude per day for the first time.

Area covered by seismic exploration is drastically reduced to 114 hectares.

1961

Anti-oil industry novel *Oficina No 1* by Miguel Otero Silva is published.

Sun drills a development well in the SVS area of the Bolívar Coastal field which has 1,843 feet of net oil sand, the thickest producing section found in Venezuela.

January 4
Ministry of Mines and Hydrocarbons Resolution 2 finally grants 140,000 hectares to the CVP.

January 21
The second Conference of OPEC ends in Caracas. Thirteen

Resolutions are adopted, notably on prices of crude oil on the international market. Qatar is accepted as the sixth Member, the Statutes are approved and Geneva is selected as headquarters of the Secretariat.

January 23
The present Constitution is adopted. Operation and administration of hydrocarbons are within the competence of the National Power; the State shall attend to the conservation of natural resources and their exploitation for the chief benefit of the Venezuelan people; "under no circumstances" can new concessions be granted, unless authorized by the National Congress.

February 13
Income Tax Law is amended. Payments by oil industry are placed on a "pay as you go" basis.

February 25
Alfredo Tarre-Murzi is appointed as first Governor for Venezuela to OPEC.

March 19
By Decree 390, exchange controls are introduced in Venezuela. Oil dollar rate continues at $1 equals 3.09 Bs.

April 15
Mata-20-1 is completed as an oil producer by Texas (Maturín basin, Oficina group, 20 km NE of West Guara field).

April 24
The national network of gas pipelines and its dependents, rights and possessions are transferred by the Venezuelan Petrochemical Institute to the CVP.

May 4
The first session of the Board of Governors of OPEC ends in Geneva. The Board meets four times a year.

May 12
9L-1, first well of the CVP, spuds in (Lamar field).

May 26
National Congress promulgates Law agreeing to the treaty signed in Baghdad establishing OPEC.

June
Fedepetrol joins the International Federation of Petroleum and Chemical Workers.

June 26-29
A "Conference of State Oil Companies of the Americas", invited by Minister Pérez Alfonzo, ends in Maracay.

June 29
The Law of Urgent Economic Measures is approved by the National Congress.

June 30
Income Tax Law is amended.
  CVP completes its first well, in the Lamar field. Minister Pérez Alfonzo attends ceremony at well-site three days later.
  Collective Contract with marine officers union signed by oil companies.

July 19
Resolution 551 of the Ministry of Mines and Hydrocarbons finally grants the national network of gasducts to the CVP.

July 26
A Law is passed embodying the 1958 Geneva Convention on the Continental Shelf.

August 15
Venezuela ratifies the International Convention of the Continental Shelf.

September 21
Mata-21-1 is completed as an oil producer by Texas (Maturín basin, Oficina group, 25 km NE of West Guara field).

October 3
The Ministry of Mines and Hydrocarbons eliminates the regulation prohibiting drilling within 1,200 metres of national reserves, free zones and "sobrantes".

November 1
The IIIrd Conference of OPEC ends in Tehran. Twelve Resolutions are approved, notably on the establishment of an Information Centre within the Secretariat and on a feasibility study of the fields within which, as far as practicable, uniformity in the practices, methods and techniques is desirable and convenient.

November 7
After three years of unsuccessful wildcatting in the Barinas basin, a new field is discovered on completion of Hato-1 by Socony (8 km sw of Silvestre field).

December 13
New areas are assigned for exploitation to the CVP.

December 31
For the first time in the development of the oil industry, there is in Venezuela a negative rate of increase of proved reserves, in the order of 475 million barrels, which cause a reduction in the volume of proved reserves.

Total crew-months of geological surface parties is drastically reduced to twelve.

1962

February 24
The Casigua-La Fría gas pipeline of the CVP is inaugurated.

March 2
In a circular letter, Ministry of Mines and Hydrocarbons reminds oil companies that if oil reservoirs extend beyond the limits of

their leases, the petroleum resources therefrom are inappropriable by them.

March 3
National Congress assigns to the CVP an additional area of almost 130,000 hectares—in the Anzoátegui, Monagas, Zulia and Barinas States.

March 12
Pres. Betancourt in a message to Congress refers to the fact that CVP has started operations.

March 19
13R-1, first CVP well in the Barinas basin, spuds in.

March 24
Pres. Betancourt, in an address opening the First Venezuelan Petroleum Congress, says private oil companies will not be nationalized, but rather will work side by side with the CVP.

April 2
Decree 723 amends Decree 580 of June 30, 1961.

April 8
The Ist Session of the IVth Conference of OPEC ends in Geneva.

May 11
Mobil completes Barquis-1A as a successful new field wildcat. This is the only new field discovery in Venezuela during the year (Maturín basin, 50 km E of Temblador field, 30 km W of Tucupita field).

June 4
Indonesia and Libya join OPEC.

June 8
The IVth Conference of OPEC ends in Geneva. Three very im-

portant Resolutions are agreed upon concerning the restoration of posted prices of oil to prior-August 1960 levels, the expensing of royalties in the Middle East and the elimination of any contributions to the marketing expenses of the companies.

September 5
Ministry of Mines and Hydrocarbons announces that gas supplied by one company to another, for reinjection, will not pay exploitation taxes.

November
Lagogás-I is inaugurated. It will reinject 170 million cubic feet of gas a day to reservoirs of the Lagunillas area of the Bolívar Coastal field.

November 25
The Ist Session of the Vth Conference of OPEC ends in Riyadh. Three Resolutions on administrative matters are approved.

November 30
Pres. Kennedy amends mandatory oil imports programme, fixing quotas on basis of production and not of demand. Exemptions for volumes imported "overland" from Canada and Mexico are introduced.

December 4
Decree 906 provides that donations in excess of Bs. 5,000 from oil companies must be approved by Ministry of Finance to be deductible for income tax purposes.

December 12
An Assistant of Pres. Kennedy and the Sub-secretary of Interior travel to Caracas to explain aspects of the imports programme.

1963

Shell completes new pool wildcat VLE-400 as the first Cretaceous producer in Lake Maracaibo (Lamar field).

January 1
President Betancourt outlines in his New Year Message the programmes to be followed in the development of the national economy and in particular of petroleum policies.

January 3
Petroleum Counsellors are appointed to the recently established Embassies in Saudi Arabia and Iran.

January 4
The Venezuelan Petroleum Corporation starts production from oil fields in the Barinas State, with an output of nearly 4,000 barrels per day.

February 12
Four-day first meeting of a Venezuelan-U.S. technical consultative group on the U.S. imports programme ends in Washington.

February 20
Presidents Betancourt of Venezuela, and Kennedy of the U.S., have an interview in Washington. There is agreement that Venezuela's interests should be acknowledged in any U.S. oil programme.

March 15
The U.S. increases by 10 per cent the Venezuelan residual oil quota.

March 29
Richmond completes Zulia 29F-1 as a small producer of heavy oil. The completion is the only important exploration development in Venezuela during the year (Maracaibo basin, 5 km SE of Los Claros field, 5 km NW of Urdaneta field).

April 4
A Consultative Meeting of OPEC is held in Geneva.

May 7
TV nation-wide debate on oil matters between Minister Pérez Alfonzo and Arturo Uslar-Pietri.

May 18
A new Collective Contract is concluded between Fedepetrol and representatives of the operating companies.

May 30
Collective Contract signed between marine workers union, represented by Federation of Workers in the Industry of Hydro-carbons and Derivatives (*Fetrahidrocarburos*), and operating oil companies.

June 5
Chamber of Deputies declares that the import policy of the United States seriously prejudices Venezuelan oil.

July 1
National Government takes over maintenance of navigation south of Cabimas.

July 4
The IInd Consultative Meeting of Heads of Delegations of OPEC ends in Geneva. Algeria, Colombia, Nigeria and Trinidad attended as observers.

August 7
New areas are assigned for exploitation to the CVP.

September 30
CVP sets up headquarters in Maracaibo. This move is considered of great significance for the economy of Zulia State.

October 9
The IIIrd Consultative Meeting of OPEC ends in Geneva.

December 1
Orderly elections, a resounding vindication of the democratic process, are held; 95 per cent go to the polls. Dr. Raúl Leoni is elected to succeed Betancourt.

December 4
The IVth Consultative Meeting of OPEC takes place in Beirut.

December 5
The Supreme Court decides in favour of Mene Grande an important legal issue concerning the disposal by the oil company of permanent installations which, at the end of the duration of a concession, would have passed free to the Government.

December 16
Manuel Pérez-Guerrero is appointed Minister of Mines and Hydrocarbons.

December 19
Minister Pérez-Guerrero announces that the Government will continue the oil policies of former Minister Pérez Alfonzo, although new and different modalities might be introduced in its application.

December 31
IInd Session of the Vth OPEC Conference ends in Riyadh. A committee is established to continue negotiations with the oil companies concerning the expensing of royalties. Studies on a project for the creation of an economic commission on crude oil prices should be prepared.

Volume of cumulative production (17,300 million barrels) exceeds volume of proved reserves (17,000 million barrels) for the first time.

1964

January 14

Texaco Maracaibo takes over the properties of Superior Oil of Venezuela.

January 18

Exchange control restrictions of 1961 are eliminated and new rate for the oil dollar is fixed at Bs. 4.40 per dollar.

January 30

Ministry of Mines and Hydrocarbons announces that oil companies will not be authorized to open new service stations.

March

OG-1, the discovery well of the Oficina field, is recompleted as a water-injection well. It had produced 1,104,921 barrels of oil in twenty seven years.

March 3

Shell Química de Venezuela, a Venezuelan corporation, is established.

March 11

In an inaugural address, Pres. Leoni reaffirms regard for present concessions and the fact that service contracts will be the basis for future development.

March 31

The Morón refinery—one of the smallest in the country—is transferred from the Petrochemical Institute to the CVP.

April 6

Tanker Esso Maracaibo, out of control due to an electric failure, collides with section of new eight-kilometre concrete bridge over Lake Maracaibo. Some 300 metres of roadway fall into the water; seven people die.

April 9
The Vth Consultative Meeting of OPEC ends in Geneva.

June 12
Closing Fedecámaras meeting, Pres. Leoni asserts national oil policies are positive and well defined and that the CVP will impulse oil activities.

July 10
The San Lorenzo refinery starts processing CVP crude.

July 14
The VIth Conference of OPEC ends in Geneva. Five Departments are established in the Secretariat (Administration, Economics, Enforcement, Public Relations and Technical) and a procedure for final negotiations with the oil companies on the question of expensing of royalties is agreed upon.

July 17
Minister Pérez-Guerrero visits Canada.

July 31
Celebration for the fiftieth anniversary of the discovery of Mene Grande oilfield.

August 13
A Collective Contract, similar to that signed by private oil companies, is signed between the CVP and Fedepetrol.

October
Seven companies join in a vast geophysical survey of the Gulf of Venezuela offshore area.

October 4
The first session of a special Consultative Meeting of OPEC is held in Beirut from September 30th to October 4th.

October 10

Lake Maracaibo bridge reopens to traffic, following partial destruction by Creole tanker.

October 28

A meeting of State oil companies of Latin America ends in Buenos Aires. CVP is represented.

November 3

Presidential Decree 187 sets out a new system for regulating the distribution of petroleum products on the domestic market. The CVP will receive one-third of the market by the end of 1968. A quota will be established for the building of gasoline stations, based on the estimated consumption. Some of the stations presently held by private companies will also be transferred to CVP.

The second session of a special Consultative Meeting of OPEC ends in Geneva.

November 5

Pres. Leoni, at the occasion of the formation of a coalition with the URD and FND political parties, says that service contracts are under discussion.

November 13

The third meeting of the technical Venezuelan-U.S. committee studying the import programme problems ends.

November 15

CVP starts construction of Morón-San Felipe-Barquisimeto gas pipeline.

November 28

VIIth OPEC Conference ends in Djakarta. Five Resolutions are passed, one of them in partial settlement of the question of expensing of royalties and another establishing an economic commission for the study of prices on the international markets.

November 29
A significant discovery is made by Signal in Lake Maracaibo with the successful completion of wildcat Centro 37-X (Centro field).

December 2
Resolution 1010 of the Ministry of Mines and Hydrocarbons sets at 107,655 m^3 the estimated demand of petroleum products on the domestic market, in connection with Decree 187.

December 8
U.S. Department of Interior announces minor changes in oil import regulations.

1965

January 22
Resolution 50 of the Ministry of Mines and Hydrocarbons assigns to the CVP the drilling of three exploratory wells in the Guanarito area (Barinas basin, 120 km NE of Barinas).

February 2
The Organizational Meeting of ARPEL (Latin American State Oil Companies Association) ends in Lima. CVP is a member.

February 10
Amendments to oil import regulations concerning emergency advances for residual fuel oil quotas are put into force by the U.S. Secretary of Interior.

February 26
Páez-4 of Varco discovers a small field (Barinas basin, 10 km W of Sinco field).

March 19
A three-day meeting at the political level of Venezuelan and U.S. officials ends. The problems of the imports programme are discussed.

May 27
Texas discovers the Bombal field on completion of new field wildcat Bombal 2-1 (Maturín basin, 60 km E of Temblador field).

July 1
Richmond becomes Chevron Oil of Venezuela.

July 13
The IXth OPEC Conference ends in Tripoli, Libya. Resolution 61 establishes, as a temporary measure for the stabilization of prices, a production programme among member countries.

August 14
Shell completes Lagunillas area inland well LS-3000 (Bolívar Coastal field).

September 1
OPEC headquarters moves to Vienna.

October 3
The First Ordinary Conference of ARPEL ends in Rio de Janeiro. The Constitution is approved. CVP and all Latin American State oil companies (except Pemex) become founder members.

October 22
Japan Gasoline Co. is winner in bidding for expansion of CVP's Morón refinery from 2,300 to 16,000 B/D.

November 26
Establishment of Petrolera Mito Juan, the first Venezuelan service company.

December 10
U.S. Pres. Johnson sets mandatory oil import quotas for 1966. The "special position" of Venezuelan oil for "Western Hemisphere security" is recognized. Allocations are granted for petrochemical plants feedstocks and also for petrochemical facilities in Puerto Rico.

December 17
The Xth OPEC Conference ends in Vienna. It is decided that posted, or reference prices, should be used as the basis for the calculation of income tax liabilities in member countries and to give full support to Libya, in connection with the attitude of certain oil companies towards the recent amendment of the Petroleum Law of that country.

December 30
Ministry of Mines and Hydrocarbons decides (*oficio* 3299) that from January 1, 1966, no discounts in excess of 10% below the posted price of residual fuel oil for export, shall be authorized.

December 31
Volume of crude petroleum produced in Venezuela since inception reaches 20,000 million barrels.

More than 400 million barrels of crude are processed during the year in Venezuelan refineries.

Area under concession is less than 3 million hectares.

1966
January 5
Production during the current week averaged 3,879,353 barrels of oil per day.

March 11
Ministry of Mines and Hydrocarbons notifies oil companies that effective April 1, maximum permissible discount on fuel oil prices will be 15 per cent off posted prices.

March 23
Ministry of Mines and Hydrocarbons issues a Resolution requiring the private oil companies to cede to the CVP, prior to the end of the year, a sufficient number of outlets to represent at least ten per cent of the companies' 1964 domestic gasoline sales.

March 30
The U.S. Department of the Interior issues regulations liberalizing the U.S. residual import programme. New quotas will be set at total requested by marketeers.

April 5
Pancoastal sells its holdings in Venezuela to Texas.

April 14
Unigás-I, giant compression plant in Lake Maracaibo, is inaugurated. It will inject 120 million cubic feet of gas per day to reservoirs of Lower Lagunillas, allowing recovery of 2,000 million barrels of oil (Bolívar Coastal field).

April 18
U.S. Administrator of Oil Import Administration issues Residual Fuel Oil Import Instructions, in accordance with Oil Import Regulations issued on March 30th by Secretary of Interior.

May 18
An agreement is signed between the CVP and the Municipal Council of Caracas, concerning the installations and rights for natural gas distribution within the city.

May 23
New York City issues regulation establishing the maximum levels of sulphur content in heavy fuel oil used in the area at 2.2% to April 1969, 2.0% to two years later, and 1% as from April 1971.

May 25
Following similar action on the part of the Chamber of Deputies, the Venezuelan Senate gives support to the national petroleum policies, in particular, the defence of prices in the international market, the tax claims, OPEC, Decree 187, fuel oil discounts limit and the service contracts approach.

May 28
Pres. Leoni inaugurates the CVP Morón-Barquisimeto 147 km gasline.

June 19
Meeting of the National Development Council, to discuss the social problem of "abandoned areas",where exploitation has gone to very low levels.

June 20
The National Energy Council is reconstituted and meets for the first time in years. It is composed of eighteen representatives of government, private industry, trade unions and political parties.

June 23
Pres. Leoni, opening the annual meeting of private investors' Fedecámaras, reiterates the "jealous" defence of the nation's natural riches. "Defence of petroleum prices and resistance to pressures of all sorts have been the permanent preoccupation of the Government and the central object of the petroleum policy."

June 26
Pres. of YPF Facundo Suárez says in Caracas that Argentina and Venezuela (YPF and CVP) could possibly reach an agreement on oil.

June 27
Meeting of Fedecámaras approves recommendations asking Government for revision of the oil policy, to allow mixed enterprises for development of petrochemicals, to spell out basis of service contracts as soon as possible.

July 11
Pres. Leoni signs the law approving the Treaty of Montevideo, indicating the intention of Venezuela to enter the Latin America Free Trade Association—LAFTA.

Law of the Venezuelan Workers Bank is enacted.

July 25
Second Ordinary Assembly of ARPEL ends in Lima. YPF of Argentina did not attend.

July 29
Resolution 860 of Ministry of Mines and Hydrocarbons orders the transfer of an additional 10 per cent of domestic gasoline sale outlets by private companies to CVP during 1966, in twelve States and the Federal District.

August 9
By Decree 598, Presidential Commission of eleven members, representing public and private sectors, is established to evaluate the present public expenditure system and, in particular, to study the function of oil revenues in the economic and social development of the country.

August 11
Collective Contract signed between Fedepetrol and major operating companies, providing for pay increases of between 10 and 12 per cent and 99 per cent stability.

August 18
Presidential Commission to evaluate public expenditures is installed by Minister of the Interior, Gonzalo Barrios. President of the Commission is former Finance Minister, Andrés Germán Otero.

September 1
The Chamber of Deputies approves a vague proposal to increase the taxes on the oil companies and to give the CVP all the domestic gasoline market.

September 8
CVP begins construction of a new gas distribution network for Caracas.

October 4
The Technical Office of the Ministry of Mines and Hydrocarbons sets definitions and regulations on reserves of oil estimates.

October 6
Min. Pérez-Guerrero announces on TV and radio national hook-up, terms of agreements with private oil companies on tax claims, introduction of reference prices and new income tax rates.

October 17
First Meeting of Representatives of OPEC National Oil Companies ends in Maracaibo. Six recommendations are approved, one of which refers to the study of ways and means of co-ordinating the entrance of the State companies into the world petroleum markets.

October 27
National Energy Council presents to Congress the basis and norms for service contracts.

October 28
Work for expansion of Morón refinery starts.

November
Creole starts operation of its Lagunillas crude dehydration plant, the world's largest.

November 25
Pres. of Fedepetrol, Luis Tovar, is appointed President of International Federation of Petroleum and Chemical Workers at end of Vth World Petroleum Congress meeting in Caracas.

December 8
The XIIth Conference of OPEC ends in Kuwait.

December 9
Venezuelan Congress approves tax bill which includes tax reform for private oil companies.

December 12
Shell Mara, largest tanker flying the Venezuelan tricolour, is christened at Puerto Miranda.

The United States Oil Import Administration amends the oil imports regulation defining refinery inputs.

The Second Ordinary Meeting of ARPEL ends in Montevideo.

December 23
New Income Tax Law (*Ley de Impuesto sobre la Renta*). The "cedular" tax is eliminated and a new rate of 52% income tax is established for net incomes of plus Bs. 28 million. For certain reinvestments in exploration, secondary recovery projects and conservation of gas, reductions of at the most 4% are possible. The effective date of the Law is January 1, 1967. It introduces the system of calculating the tax liabilities on the basis of reference prices, which increase gradually over a period of five years to predetermined levels.

December 29
CVP inaugurates its 100th service station.

1967

January 3
José Antonio Mayobre is sworn in as Minister of Mines and Hydrocarbons.

January 9
Venezuela adheres to the Montevideo Treaty, LAFTA (Latin American Free Trade Association).

January 19
New York-New Jersey Inter-state Air Pollution Abatement Conference recommends that fuel oil containing more than 1% sulphur by weight should not be used as of October 1, 1969 by

steam or electric power companies, nor heating oil containing more than 0.3 % sulphur by weight.

February 3
Minister of Finance, Morales-Crespo, signs with Shell and Creole the agreements negotiated by Mines Minister, Pérez-Guerrero, introducing reference prices for the next five years and accepting income tax of 51 per cent (formerly 47.5 per cent). Also agreed, tax claims for previous years, $85 million for Creole and $55.5 million for Shell, payable one-third on signature, one-third in nine months and one-third in eighteen months.

February 21
Mito Juan sets up subsidiary to acquire two small blocks of concessions in the Maturín basin, southeast of Oficina.

February 24
A Seminar on the Oil Industry in Latin America, sponsored by the Economic Commission for Latin America, ends in Santiago de Chile. Representatives of Venezuela submit papers on hydrocarbon reserves, conservation, prices of oil in the international markets and financing.

April 8
During the 7th World Petroleum Congress in Mexico City, the CVP presents three papers on the geology of the unexplored Gulf of Venezuela basin, the hydrocarbon resources of the tar belt of the Maturin basin and the exploration drilling programme at Guanarito.

April 12
Pres. Leoni discusses with United States President Johnson in Punta del Este, problems of mutual interest, among them sulphur content of Venezuelan crudes and imports to the U.S.

April 14
The Conference of Presidents of States of the American republics

ends in Punta del Este. It is proposed to integrate in a hemispheric common market by 1980.

April 25
The U.S. Department of Interior extends for three years the informal arrangement by which 30,000 barrels per day of Mexican oil enters the United States under the "overland" exemption provisions of the mandatory oil import control programme.

In a speech to the Ist National Convention of Exporters, Minister Mayobre declares that he is optimistic regarding the future of the petroleum industry but that no one should expect a new boom, as in past years.

April 27
The CVP completes Mingo-1 as a new field discovery, south of Silvestre. It is the southernmost producer in the Barinas basin.

May 4
Managing Director, Sáder Pérez, announces that the CVP might run out of gasoline. Supply agreements had elapsed and oil companies were now asking for a three-fold increase in prices.

May 5
National Congress President, Luis A. Dubuc, announces Mines and Hydrocarbons Commission is studying possibility of amending 1943 Hydrocarbons Law, to facilitate procedures on future service contracts.

May 8
CVP and Shell sign an agreement on the supply of gasoline to CVP pump stations for three months.

May 10
The annual meeting of private investors, Fedecámaras, again sharply attacks national oil policy, following publication of some newspaper articles in the Caracas press.

May 12
Pres. Leoni stresses national oil policy in a speech to the Nation. He says the Government would not accept any lowering of the reference prices and that the prospects of finding new reserves—in southern Lake Maracaibo, Gulf of Venezuela and the tar belt—are great.

May 13
The Economic Commission for Latin America ends its 12th Annual Meeting, held in Caracas. Reports on a seminar on oil economics for Latin America, held during February in Santiago, are discussed.

May 22
CVP completes Caipe-1 as a new field discovery. It is the northernmost producer in the Barinas basin.

May 23
Pres. Lowry of Creole informs the Senate Commission of Mines and Hydrocarbons that his company is not interested in signing service contracts with the CVP.

May 26
Creole submits to the Ministry of Mines and Hydrocarbons a proposal to build a $100 million desulphurization plant.

May 31
Former Development Minister, Egaña, proposes to the National Economic Council that mixed companies should take over exploitation of concessions expiring in 1983.

Minister Mayobre defends petroleum national policy in a debate in the Senate.

June 5
Israel-Arab war. Suez Canal is closed two days later; production in Arab exporting countries partially interrupted.

June 9
Thirteenth Conference of OPEC postponed.

June 12
Venezuelan officials declare country will not behave with "mercantilist spirit" in Middle East crisis and that developments have shown "geopolitical strategic value of Venezuelan oil".

June 17
CVP makes first delivery of Boscán crude (75,000 barrels) to a private oil company, at Bajo Grande terminal.

June 25
Ministry of Mines and Hydrocarbons authorizes the building of thirty-five new service stations during 1967; thirty-two of the total thirty-five are given to the CVP (all of those in the highly populated areas).

July 17
A Proclamation of the U.S. President is issued to enhance ability to provide adequate supplies of low sulphur residual fuel oil to use as fuel and to allow entrance into mandatory imports programme of new importers.

July 18
It is reported that CVP exports first shipment of oil, 75,000 barrels to England.

July 20
National Congress passes bill amending 1943 Hydrocarbons Law. Service contracts may be negotiated by the Ministry of Mines and Hydrocarbons or by the CVP, on terms which should result more favourably for the nation than those of existing concessions. Duration of contracts is five years for exploration and twenty for development.

Law governing special agreements related to hydrocarbons desulphurizing is passed by National Congress, to provide

159

special reference prices for up to ten years for low-sulphur petroleum crudes and products. Bill aims at allowing Venezuelan oil and products to meet more rigid requirements of U.S. consumers.

July 31
Production during the month averaged 3,750,212 barrels per day, an all-time monthly record.

August
Sinclair brings on stream 5,000 barrels per day refinery in Sinco field (Barinas basin) to meet local requirements of gasoline, kerosene and diesel oil.

August 14
Executive Decree orders oil companies to cede to the CVP enough service stations to permit the national agency to cover one-tenth of volume of gasolines sold in domestic market during 1966.

August 17
Industry celebrates, in San Lorenzo, fiftieth anniversary of refining operations in Venezuela.

August 18
Bases for regional common market of "Andes countries" (Colombia, Chile, Ecuador, Peru and Venezuela) are agreed upon in Caracas.

August 28
On the occasion of signing an agreement for integration of major fertilizer plants in Venezuela (El Tablazo) and Colombia (Barranquilla), president of Colombian Petroquímica del Atlántico, Jorge Barco, announces plans for construction of gasoline by the CVP from Lake Maracaibo to Barranquilla.

September 9
Sun produces 500-millionth barrel of oil from its 1957 concession.

September 11
Sun, as operator for itself and two other groups of associates, announces construction of one gas compression and extraction plant in BCF's Lama area, and of a natural gas liquids fractionating plant in Bajo Grande.

September 17
OPEC holds Extraordinary (XIIIth) Conference in Rome.

September 26
Venezuela's Supreme Court hands down decision supporting Ministry of Mines and Hydrocarbons view that concessionaire companies are obliged to submit all information the Ministry considers necessary to ensure full understanding of oil development in the country.

September 27
CVP will accept bids for joint exploration and development in the South Lake Maracaibo offshore area, under service contracts.

CVP Managing Director Sáder-Pérez announces start of production at 8,000 barrels per day from Mata (Maturín basin) to cover volume sold to Petrobrás. It is the first important sale of the CVP in world markets and Company is proud "of having maintained prices". Sáder-Pérez also announces supply of gasolines to the CVP stations is assured, as agreement with Creole, Shell, Mene Grande, Texas, Mobil and Phillips is signed.

September 28
The Venezuelan Petrochemical Institute and Commonwealth Oil Refining of Puerto Rico disclose co-operation plans for developing broad-based petrochemical industry in Venezuela, Puerto Rico and perhaps elsewhere in Latin America.

U.S. Government increases fuel quotas.

October 2
Shell announces plans for installing a $23 million desulphurization plant at Cardón.

October 21
Third General Assembly of ARPEL ends in Caracas. It is decided to move headquarters to Montevideo and to study problems of economic integration within LAFTA, in the field of hydrocarbons.

November 1
Minister Mayobre declares Venezuela cannot always be dependent on what the United States will or will not do on oil imports. He also says that domestic political considerations are the major stumbling block for the elimination of discriminatory provisions in the U.S. import programme, and that the proposed bills are an expression of a kind of economic isolationism.

November 3
The CVP asks interested foreign oil companies to participate in sharing information from seismic survey in southern Lake Maracaibo area.

November 8
Presidents of three large U.S. gas transmission companies visit President Leoni and express a desire eventually to purchase, in liquid form, 600 million cubic feet a day of natural gas.

November 9
Negotiations on a technical level resume between Venezuela and the U.S., referring to the new threat on oil trade.

November 10
The Second Meeting of Representatives of the National Oil Companies of OPEC ends in Djakarta. CVP attends. It is decided to authorize the commissioning of a study on the joint co-operation among the N.O.C.s in the international market.

November 23
National Congress unanimously backs actions of Ministry of Mines and Hydrocarbons in the U.S. against proposed restrictive legislation and urges Latin American Parliament to take unified stand on the matter.

November 29
Fourteenth OPEC Conference ends in Vienna. It is decided to pre-
pare new studies to make production programme practical and
effective and to admit Abu Dhabi as ninth member.

December 1
First shipment of 100,000 barrels of CVP oil to Brazil.
    Chairman of U.S. Federal Power Commission visits Ministry of
Mines and Hydrocarbons, probably to discuss possibility of
exporting liquefied natural gas to the U.S.

December 4
A company for the distribution of natural gas is incorporated in
Barquisimeto. The CVP and private interests participate.

December 7
Shell puts on stream 30,000 barrels per day hydrodesulphurization
unit in Curaçao refinery.

December 19
Senate transfer to the CVP 200,000 hectares in the southern lake
Maracaibo area and 100,000 hectares in the Paraguaná area.
    Shell announces readiness to negotiate desulphurizing projects
in Cardón.

December 26
The CVP announces exports of one million barrels of oil to
Yugoslavia starting in January 1968.

December 29
The CVP and Ecopetrol, the Colombian State oil agency, agree in
Bogotá on non-overlapping geophysical surveys in the northern
area of the Gulf of Venezuela.

December 31

The Government and Creole sign first agreement to build desulphurizing plant at Amuay. The unit valued at Bs 528 million, will process 100,000 barrels per day. It is largest plant in the world.

The CVP signs an agreement to supply iron-ore new plant of Orinoco Mining with natural gas. The CVP will build gas line from Mobil's Guario field to Guayana plant.

Western Venezuelan fields produce for the first time more than 1,000 million barrels in a single year.

APPENDIX 1. LOCATION OF VENEZUELAN FIELDS

FIELD	LOCATION
Abundancia	Falcón basin; 120 km SE of Coro, 25 km SW of El Mene de Acosta fd.
Acema	Maturín basin, Oficina group, 20 km E of Aguasay fd.
Adas	Maturín basin, Oficina group, 15 km S of Oritupano fd.
AdM-101	Maturín basin, Oficina group, 5 km W of Oritupano fd.
Adobe	Maturín basin, Oficina group, 20 km W of Oritupano fd.
Adrales	Maturín basin, Oficina group, 10 km W of Oritupano fd.
Aguasay	Maturín basin, Oficina group, 40 km NE of West Guara fd.
Algarrobo	Maturín basin, 7 km SW of Oficina group–Yopales fd.
La Alquitrana	Maracaibo basin, southern end, near Colombian border, 15 km W of San Cristóbal
Alturitas	Maracaibo basin, 140 km SW of Maracaibo
Amana	Maracaibo basin, 70 km NW of Maracaibo
Anaco	Maturín basin, Anaco group, 15 km NE of El Roble fd.
Aníbal	Maturín basin, 40 km W of Oficina group–Elotes fd.
Apamate	Maturín basin, Anaco group, 5 km W of El Toco
Araibel	Maturín basin, Oficina group, 25 km NE of Chimire fd.
Avipa	Maturín basin, 8 km W of Jusepín fd.
Barbacoas	Maturín basin, 30 km N of Las Mercedes fd.
Barquis	Maturín basin; 50 km E of Temblador fd., 30 km W of Tucupita fd.
Los Barrosos	Maracaibo basin, 5 km N of Mene Grande fd.
Barso	Maturín basin, 100 km ESE of Las Mercedes fd.
Barúa	Maracaibo basin, 8 km SSW of Mene Grande fd.

FIELD	LOCATION
Belén	Maturín basin, 15 km s of Las Mercedes fd.
Bella Vista	Maturín basin, 55 km SE of Las Mercedes fd.
Boca	Maturín basin, Oficina group, 10 km N of Chimire fd.
Boca Ricoa	Falcón basin, 15 km NE of Cumarebo fd.
Bolívar Coastal	Maracaibo basin; extends for some 100 km along eastern shore of Lake Maracaibo; different producing areas discovered far spaced one of the other over period of decades (Ambrosio, La Rosa, Cabimas, Punta Benítez, Tía Juana, Lagunillas, Pueblo Viejo, Bachaquero); deeper horizons discovered offshore designated by letters and serial number of discovery well (LL-370, VL-1, LL-453, TJ-319); areas discovered during last decade also important (Ceuta, Lama, SVS); old boundaries between areas not based on geological conditions, so that it is quite incorrect to refer to a *Lagunillas field* or *Bachaquero field;* centre of development of Venezuelan petroleum industry; field—largest in the world—is usually referred to in industry jargon as BCF
Bombal	Maturín basin; 60 km E of Temblador fd., 25 km w of Tucupita fd.
Boscán	Maracaibo basin, 50 km sw of Maracaibo
Bucaral	Maturín basin; 10 km SE of Anaco group–San Joaquín fd., 10 km NW of Oficina group–Mapiri fd.
Budare	Maturín basin, Oficina group, 15 km sw of Elotes fd.
Cachipo	Maturín basin, 10 km s of Quiriquire fd.
Cagigal	Maturín basin, 120 km NE of Las Mercedes fd.
Caico Seco	Maturín basin, Oficina group, 35 km NW of Oficina fd.
Caipe	Barinas basin, 5 km N of Silvestre fd.
Cantaura	Maturín basin, 10 km N of Mapiri fd.
Capacho	Maturín basin, 5 km w of Tacat fd.
Caracoles	Maturín basin, Oficina group, 5 km s of Caico Seco fd.
Los Caritos	Maturín basin, 40 km NE of Temblador fd.
Casca	Maturín basin, 35 km NW of Anaco group–Sta. Ana fd.

FIELD	LOCATION
Cascadas	Maturín basin, 25 km WNW of Anaco group—El Toco fd.
Casón	Maturín basin, 30 km NW of Anaco group—El Toco fd.
CaZ-501	Maturín basin, Oficina group, 10 km NW of Caico Seco fd.
La Ceiba	Maturín basin, 25 km NE of Anaco group—Sta. Rosa fd.
La Ceibita	Maturín basin, Oficina group, 15 km N of Soto fd.
Central Guara	Maturín basin, Oficina group, 20 km NE of Oficina fd.
Centro	Maracaibo basin, offshore in Lake Maracaibo; 80 km S of Maracaibo, 15 km S of nearest BCF production
Cerro Pelado	Maturín basin, 30 km NE of Sta. Rosa fd.
Chaparrito	Maturín basin, 4 km S of El Toco fd.
Chaparro	Maturín basin, 15 km W of El Toco fd.
Chimire	Maturín basin, Oficina group, 15 km N of Oficina fd.
CL	Maracaibo basin, offshore in Lake Maracaibo; 100 km S of Maracaibo, 30 km W of Ceuta area of BCF
Los Claros	Maracaibo basin, 60 km SW of Maracaibo
Cocomón	Maturín basin, 75 km E of Las Mercedes fd.
La Concepción	Maracaibo basin, 20 km W of Maracaibo
Coporo	Maturín basin, 110 km SE of Las Mercedes fd.
Las Cruces	Maracaibo basin, Tarra group, near Colombian border, 255 km SW of Maracaibo
Cumarebo	Falcón basin, 30 km E of Coro
Dación	Maturín basin, Oficina group, 20 km E of East Guara fd.
Dakoa	Maturín basin, 40 km E of Las Mercedes fd.
East Aguasay	Maturín basin, Oficina group, 20 km E of Aguasay fd.
East Caico	Maturín basin, Oficina group, 10 km NE of Caico Seco fd.
East Guanoco	Maturín basin, 20 km ESE of Guanoco fd.
East Guara	Maturín basin, Oficina group, 30 km NE of Oficina fd.

FIELD	LOCATION
East Mapiri	Maturín basin, Oficina group, 5 km E of Mapiri fd.
East Soto	Matur n basin, Oficina group, 5 km E of Soto fd.
Elotes	Maturín basin, Oficina group, 50 km W of Oficina fd.
Ensenada	Maracaibo basin, 35 km S of Maracaibo
Esquina	Maturín basin, Oficina group, 10 km SW of Chimire fd.
Estero	Barinas basin, 3 km N of Silvestre fd.
Finca	Maturín basin, Oficina group, 30 km NW of Oficina fd.
La Freitera	Maturín basin, Oficina group, 35 km N of Chimire fd.
Freites	Maturín basin, Oficina group, 15 km N of Chimire fd.
Galán	Maturín basin, 8 km N of Mapiri fd.
Ganso	Maturín basin, Oficina group, 10 km S of East Guara fd.
GG-401	Maturín basin, Oficina group, 8 km E of West Guara fd.
GM-2X	Maturín basin, Oficina group, 10 km S of West Guara fd.
GM-4X	Maturín basin, Oficina group, 8 km W of West Guara fd.
Gozo	Maturín basin, 50 km SE of Las Mercedes fd.
Grico	Maturín basin, 40 km W of Las Mercedes fd.
Guanoco	Maturín basin, 60 km NE of Maturín
Guario	Maturín basin, Anaco group, 15 km NE of San Joaquín fd.
Guavinita	Maturín basin, 30 km SW of Las Mercedes fd.
Güere	Maturín basin, Oficina group, 40 km NW of Chimire fd.
Güico	Maturín basin, Oficina group, 5 km W of West Guara fd.
Hato	Barinas basin, 8 km SW of Silvestre fd.
Hombre Pintado	Falcón basin, 16 km NE of El Mene de Mauroa fd.
Icaco	Maturín basin, Oficina group, 5 km S of Caico Seco fd.

FIELD	LOCATION
Icón	Maturín basin, Oficina group, 15 km sw of Caico Seco fd.
Ida	Maturín basin, 10 km nw of Elotes fd.
Inca	Maturín basin, Oficina group, 7 km sw of Caico Seco fd.
Ipire	Maturín basin; 120 km se of Las Mercedes fd., 120 km w of Oficina fd.
Ira	Maturín basin, 25 km w of Oficina group–Caico Seco fd.
Iris	Maturín basin, 20 km sw of Güere fd.
Isla	Maturín basin, Oficina group, 10 km sw of Caico Seco fd.
Isleño	Maturín basin, 20 km se of Temblador fd.
Jobal	Maturín basin, 70 km ne of Las Mercedes fd.
Jobo	Maturín basin, 25 km sw of Temblador fd.
Juanita	Maturín basin, Oficina group, 5 km w of Elotes fd.
Junta	Maturín basin, Oficina group, 10 km w of Oritupano fd.
Jusepín	Maturín basin, 35 km w of Maturín; single trap, 35 km sw/ne, max. 7 km across, to which different names used by various operators (Sta. Bárbara, Mulata, Muri, Travieso, W. Travieso)
Kaki	Maturín basin, Oficina group, 8 km w of Mapiri fd.
Lago	Maracaibo basin, offshore Lake Maracaibo, 100 km s of Maracaibo, 10 km e of Lama area, Bolívar Coastal fd.
Laloma	Maturín basin, 5 km e of San Roque fd.
Lamar	Maracaibo basin, offshore Lake Maracaibo, 110 km s of Maracaibo, 30 km s of Lama area of Bolívar Coastal fd.
Largo	Maturín basin, 15 km n of Oficina group–Soto fd.
Lazo	Maturín basin, Oficina group, 20 km e of Lobo fd.
Lechozo	Maturín basin, 25 km nw of Las Mercedes fd.
Leguas	Maturín basin, Oficina group, 12 km e of East Guara fd.

FIELD	LOCATION
Lejos	Maturín basin, Oficina group, 25 km E of East Guara fd.
Leona	Maturín basin, Oficina group, 25 km NE of East Guara fd.
Lestes	Maturín basin, Oficina group, 5 km NE of Lobo fd.
Levas	Maturín basin, Oficina group, 25 km SE of East Guara fd.
Libro	Maturín basin, Oficina group, 10 km E of Lobo fd.
Lido	Maturín basin, Oficina group, 15 km NE of East Guara fd.
Limón	Maturín basin, Oficina group, 15 km N of East Guara fd.
Lobo	Maturín basin, Oficina group, 30 km E of East Guara fd.
Lustro	Maturín basin, Oficina group, 3 km S of Lobo fd.
Macoa	Maracaibo basin, 110 km SW of Maracaibo
Mahomal	Maturín basin, 90 km ESE of Las Mercedes fd.
El Mamón	see *Urumaco*
Los Manueles	Maracaibo basin, Tarra group, 15 km N of Las Cruces fd.
Los Mangos	Maturín basin, Oficina group, 15 km NW of Caico Seco fd.
Manresa	Maturín basin, 25 km N of Jusepín fd.
Mapiri	Maturín basin, Oficina group, 25 km N of Chimire fd.
Maporal	Barinas basin, 8 km N of Silvestre fd.
Mapuey	Maturín basin, Oficina group, 10 km W of Caico Seco fd.
Mara	Maracaibo basin; 35 km NW of Maracaibo, 20 km NE of La Paz fd.
Mata	Maturín basin, Oficina group; various fields, 20 km N and 25 km NE of West Guara fd.
Mata Grande	Maturín group, 10 km W of Sta. Bárbara area of Jusepín fd.
Maulpa	Maturín basin, 10 km N of nearest Oficina fd. (Soto)
Media	Falcón basin, 7 km NE of El Mene de Mauroa fd.
Melones	Maturín basin, Oficina group, 35 km SE of East Guara fd.

FIELD	LOCATION
El Mene de Acosta	Falcón basin, 150 km SE of Coro
Mene Grande	Maracaibo basin, 20 km SE of Bolívar Coastal fd., Machango area
El Menito	Maracaibo basin, 5 km N of Mene Grande fd.
Las Mercedes	Maturín basin, 150 km S of Caracas, 360 km ESE of Maturín
Merey	Maturín basin, Oficina group, 35 km SE of Oficina fd.
Miga	Maturín basin, Oficina group, 30 km SE of Oficina fd.
Mingo	Barinas basin, 10 km S of Sinco fd.
Misoa	Maracaibo basin, 7 km N of Mene Grande fd.
Monal	Maturín basin, 45 km E of Las Mercedes fd.
Monte Claro	Falcón basin; 170 km SW of Coro, 40 km E of El Mene de Mauroa fd.
Morichal	Maturín basin, 40 km SW of Temblador fd.
Motatán	Maracaibo basin, 10 km SE of Mene Grande fd.
Nardo	Maturín basin, Oficina group, 20 km NE of West Guara fd.
Netick	Maracaibo basin, 10 km N of La Paz fd.
Nidos	Maturín basin, Oficina group, 3 km N of Chimire fd.
Nieblas	Maturín basin, Oficina group, 15 km NE of West Guara fd.
Nigua	Maturín basin, Oficina group, 25 km NE of West Guara fd.
Nipa	Maturín basin, Oficina group, 10 km N of West Guara fd.
North Cachama	Maturín basin, Oficina group, 7 km W of Chimire fd.
North Chimire	Maturín basin, Oficina group, 8 km NE of Chimire fd.
North Guara	Maturín basin, Oficina group, 6 km N of West Guara fd.
North Lamar	Maracaibo basin, 15 km N of Lamar fd., 15 km S of Lama area of Bolívar Coastal fd.
North Nipa	Maturín basin, Oficina group, 5 km N of Nipa fd.
North Oficina	Maturín basin, Oficina group, 8 km N of Oficina fd.
North Oscurote	Maturín basin, Oficina group, 5 km N of Oscurote fd.
North Santa Rosa	Maturín basin, Anaco group, 15 km NE of Sta. Rosa fd.

FIELD	LOCATION
North Soto	Maturín basin, Oficina group, 10 km NW of Soto fd.
North Yopales	Maturín basin, Oficina group, 20 km W of Oficina fd.
North Zumo	Maturín basin, Oficina group, 5 km N of Zumo fd.
Oca	Maturín basin, Oficina group, 20 km SE of Oficina fd.
Oficina	Maturín basin; area is roughly oval, extending for a maximum of 170 km from east to west and 80 km from north to south; identification of reservoir units difficult, as there always some arbitrariness arises; Oficina field proper 150 km SW of Maturín, few km W of geographical centre of group area
Oleos	Maturín basin, Oficina group, 20 km E of Oveja fd.
Las Ollas	Maturín basin, 35 km W nearest Anaco group fd. (El Toco)
Oritupano	Maturín basin, Oficina group, 40 km E of Leona fd.
Orocual	Maturín basin; 8 km NE of Jusepín fd., 20 km SW of Quiriquire fd.
Oscurote	Maturín basin, Oficina group, 25 km NE of West Guara fd.
Ostra	Maturín basin, Oficina group, 15 km SE of Oficina fd.
Oveja	Maturín basin, Oficina group, 20 km S of Oficina fd.
Páez	Barinas basin, 15 km W of Silvestre fd.
Palacio	Maturín basin, 25 km SSW of Las Mercedes fd.
Las Palmas	Falcón basin; 130 km SW of Coro, 40 km NE of El Mene de Mauroa fd.
Palmita	Barinas basin, 5 km N of Silvestre fd.
Pato	Maturín basin, 15 km E of Anaco group–Sta. Rosa fd.
La Paz	Maracaibo basin, 40 km W of Maracaibo
Pedernales	Maturín basin, 100 km NNE of Maturín
Pelayo	Maturín basin, Oficina group, 35 km E of East Guara fd.
Pilón	Maturín basin, 10 km S of Temblador fd.
Piragua	Maturín basin, 40 km SW of Las Mercedes fd.
Pirital	Maturín basin, 5 km W of Jusepín fd.
Placer	Maturín basin, 50 km NE of Las Mercedes fd.
Posa	Maturín basin, offshore in gulf of Paria, 30 km NE of Pedernales fd.

FIELD	LOCATION
Pradera	Maturín basin, Oficina group, 20 km NW of Oficina fd.
Punzón	Maturín basin, 30 km W of Las Mercedes fd.
Quiamare	Maturín basin, 40 km N of Anaco group—Sta. Rosa fd.
Quiriquire	Maturín basin, 25 km N of Maturín
Quiroz	Maracaibo basin, 40 km E of Ambrosio area of Bolívar Coastal fd., 25 km S of El Mene de Mauroa fd.
Retumbo	Maturín basin, 130 km SE of Las Mercedes fd., 110 km W of Oficina fd.
Rincón	Maturín basin, Anaco group, 10 km E of Sta. Ana fd.
Río de Oro	Maracaibo basin, in Colombian border, 225 km SW of Maracaibo
El Roble	Maturín basin, Anaco group, 12 km NE of San Joaquín fd.
Roblote	Maturín basin, 25 km W of El Toco fd.
Rosal	Maturín basin, 10 km N of Anaco group—Sta. Rosa fd.
Rosario (El)	Maturín basin, 190 km SW of Maracaibo, 50 km N of Tarra group of fields
Rositas	Maturín basin, 35 km SE of Las Mercedes fd.
Ruiz	Maturín basin, 45 km SE of Las Mercedes fd.
Sabán	Maturín basin, 65 km E of Las Mercedes fd.
El Salto	Maturín basin; 25 km E of Oficina group—Oritupano fd., 45 km NW of Temblador fd.
San Joaquín	Maturín basin, Anaco group, 150 km SE of Maturín
San José	Maracaibo basin, 110 km SW of Maracaibo
San Roque	Maturín basin, Anaco group, 15 km W of San Joaquín
Santa Ana	Maturín basin, Anaco group, 15 km SW of San Joaquín fd.
Santa Rosa	Maturín basin, Anaco group, 25 km NE of San Joaquín fd.
Sanvi	Maturín basin, 12 km NW of Oficina group—Elotes fd.

FIELD	LOCATION
Sapo	Maturín basin, Oficina group, 3 km SE of Mapiri fd.
Sibucara	Maracaibo basin, 5 km SW of Maracaibo, although portions of the proved area of the fd. are within the city limits
Silván	Barinas basin, 10 km NW of Silvestre fd.
Silvestre (San)	Barinas basin, 35 km SE of Barinas
Sinco	Barinas basin, 5 km S of Silvestre fd.
Socororo	Maturín basin, Oficina group, 15 km W of Yopales fd.
Soto	Maturín basin, Oficina group, 20 km N of Chimire fd.
South Esquina	Maturín basin, Oficina group, 10 km NW of Oficina fd.
South Güico	Maturín basin, Oficina group, 10 km S of Güico fd.
South Maracaibo	Maracaibo basin, 15 km S of Maracaibo
South Yopales	Maturín basin, Oficina group, 20 km S of Yopales fd.
Soyas	Maturín basin, Oficina group, 15 km N of Chimire fd.
Tacat	Maturín basin, 10 km W of Sta. Bárbara area, Jusepín fd.
Tácata	Maturín basin, 8 km W of Tacat fd.
Tagua	Maturín basin, Oficina group, 10 km N of Caico Seco fd.
Tamán	Maturín basin, 60 km NE of Las Mercedes fd.
Tascabaña	Maturín basin, Oficina group, 10 km W of Chimire fd.
Temblador	Maturín basin, 100 km S of Maturín
Texas	Maturín basin, 10 km ENE of Tucupita fd.
Tiguaje	Falcón basin, 130 km SW of Coro
El Toco	Maturín basin, Anaco group, 20 km W of Sta. Ana fd.
Totumo	Maracaibo basin, 85 km W of Maracaibo, 40 km SW of La Paz fd.
Trico	Maturín basin, Oficina group, 20 km W of Oficina fd.
Tucupido	Maturín basin, 60 km NE of Las Mercedes fd.
Tucupita	Maturín basin, 80 km E of Temblador fd.
UD-41	Maracaibo basin, offshore in Lake Maracaibo, 45 km S of Maracaibo

FIELD	LOCATION
Uracoa	Maturín basin, 30 km E of Temblador fd.
Urdaneta	Maracaibo basin, along western shore Lake Maracaibo, 60 km s of Maracaibo
Urumaco	Falcón basin, 70 km wsw of Coro
Valle	Maturín basin, 45 km SE of Las Mercedes fd.
La Vieja	Maturín basin, 35 km NE of Sta. Rosa fd.
West Guara	Maturín basin, Oficina group, 20 km NE of Oficina fd.
West Güico	Maturín basin, Oficina group, 5 km w of Güico fd.
West Nipa	Maturín basin, Oficina group, 5 km w of Nipa fd.
West Tarra	Maracaibo basin, Tarra group, 15 km sw of Las Cruces fd.
Yopales	Maturín basin, Oficina group, 20 km sw of Oficina fd.
Yucal	Maturín basin, 60 km N of Las Mercedes fd.
Zapatos	Maturín basin, Oficina group, 40 km NE of Chimire fd.
Zeta	Maturín basin, Oficina group, 30 km N of West Guara fd.
Zorro	Maturín basin, Oficina group, 10 km N of Zumo fd.
Zumo	Maturín basin, Oficina group, 30 km NE of West Guara fd.
1-MXZ	Maracaibo basin, 25 km N of La Paz fd.
29F-1	Maracaibo basin, 5 km SE of Los Claros fd., 5 km NW of Urdaneta fd.

APPENDIX 2. OILFIELDS IN THE OFICINA GROUP

Acema	La Freitera	Lustro	Oritupano
Adas	Freites	Los Mangos	Oscurote
AdM-101	Ganso	Mapiri	Ostra
Adobe	GG-401	Mapuey	Oveja
Adrales	GM-2X	Mata	Pelayo
Aguasay	GM-4X	Melones	Pradera
Araibel	Güere	Merey	Sapo
Boca	Güico	Miga	Socororo
Budare	Icón	Nardo	Soto
Caico Seco	Inca	Nidos	South Esquina
Caracoles	Isla	Nieblas	South Güico
CaZ-501	Juanita	Nigua	South Yopales
La Ceibita	Junta	Nipa	Soyas
Central Guara	Kaki	North Cachama	Tagua
Chimire	Lazo	North Chimire	Tascabaña
Dación	Leguas	North Guara	Trico
East Aguasay	Lejos	North Nipa	West Guara
East Caico	Leona	North Oficina	West Güico
East Guara	Lestes	North Oscurote	West Nipa
East Mapiri	Levas	North Soto	Yopales
East Soto	Libro	North Yopales	Zapatos
Elotes	Lido	North Zumo	Zeta
Esquina	Limón	Oca	Zorro
Finca	Lobo	Oleos	Zumo

APPENDIX 3. OILFIELDS BY YEAR OF DISCOVERY

	1880	
La Alquitrana		
	1913	
Guanoco		
	1914	
Mene Grande	Totumo	
	1915	
Río de Oro		
	1916	
Las Cruces		
	1917	
Bolívar Coastal		
	1918	
Misoa		
	1921	
El Mene de Mauroa		
	1922	
Los Barrosos		
	1923	
La Paz	El Menito	
	1925	
La Concepción		
	1926	
Monte Claro	Urumaco	
	1927	
Los Manueles	El Mene de Acosta	Hombre Pintado
	1928	
Amana	Quiriquire	Las Palmas
	1929	
Netick	Media	

1931		
Cumarebo		

1932		
Pirital		

1933		
Orocual	Pedernales	

1936		
Temblador	Santa Ana	

1937		
Merey	Pilón	Uracoa
Oficina	Yopales	

1938		
Leona	Jusepín	

1939		
Algarrobo	San Joaquín	El Roble

1940		
Los Caritos	Socororo	Guario
North Oficina		

1941		
Santa Rosa	Trico	Las Mercedes

1942		
West Guara	Quiamare	Anaco
East Guara	Oveja	

1943		
North Yopales	Ostra	

1944		
Güico		

1945		
Mara	GM-2X	Avipa
Tucupita	Capacho	Nipa

1946		
Caico Seco	GM-4X	Grico
West Güico	La Ceiba	South Güico
Ensenada	Mata Grande	Boscán
Palacio	Macoa	Tucupido

	1947	
Pelayo	Lechozo	West Tarra
Valle 13	Punzón	Sabán
	1948	
Chimire	(San) Silvestre	El Toco
San José	Guavinita	Inca
Ganso	Placer	Aragua
Sibucara		
	1949	
San Roque	Silván	Tamán
Ruiz	Mapiri	Piragua
Soto	Freites	Pradera
	1950	
Belén	Oritupano	Los Mangos
Dación	Tagua	La Vieja
Güere	Alturitas	Barbacoas
	1951	
Cerro Pelado	Boca	Monal
Cocomón	Laloma	East Soto
Quirz	Chaparro	Central Guara
Tascabaña	GG-401	Apamate
Esquina	East Caico	Mata 2
Mata 1	1-MXZ	Dakoa 8
	1952	
Retumbo	East Guanoco	Mata 5
Cantaura	CaZ-501	Oscurote
Bella Vista	Rincón 5	Punzón 7
East Mapiri	Mata 3	South Esquina
Tácata	Caracoles	Roblote
North Cachama	Soto	Lejos
Motatán	Sapo	
	1953	
North Chimire	North Oscurote	North Soto
Rositas	Mata 4	South Yopales
Sinco	Tiguaje	Jobo
Mapuey	La Ceibita	Tacat
Rincón 7	Junta 11	Nigua
Zorro	Zeta	

Adobe	Casca	Kaki
Oca	East Pilón	

1954

Zumo	Isla	Nardo
Cagigal	Ariabel	Coporo
Nieblas	Mahomal	Elotes
Limón	Lido	Nidos
Mata 8	Dakoa 10	Manresa
West Nipa	Casón	

1955

AdM-101	Urdaneta	Dakoa 16
Valle 16	Aníbal	Mata 9
Boca Ricoa	Mata 12	South Maracaibo
Oleos	Mata 11	Melones
Aguasay	Zapatos	Soyas

1956

Mata 13	Juanita	Adas
Pato	Texas 14	Gozo
Libro	North Zumo	Adrales
Finca	Leguas	Levas
Aguasay 3	Lustro	Leste
Icaco		

1957

Mata 14	Chaparrito 5	Valle 3
North Nipa	La Freitera	Ira
Miga	Galán	CL
UD-41	Cachipo	Grúas
Los Claros	Palmita	

1958

El Salto	Rosal	Cascadas
POSA 112	Bucaral	North Lamar
Ipire 2	Maporal	Mata 17
Lago	Mata 19	Morichal
Valle 11	Lamar	Estero
Largo		

1959		
Sanvi 5	Lazo	Barso
Dakoa 20	Budare	Maulpa
(El) Rosario	Icón	Ida
1960		
Jobal	Iris	POSA 117
Acema		
1961		
Mata 20	Mata 21	Hato
1962		
Barquis		
1963		
29F-1		
1965		
Bombal		
1967		
Mingo	Caipe	

APPENDIX 4. 'GIANT' OILFIELDS DATA

Giant Field	Year Discovered	Year Recognized	Year Produced its 100 millionth barrel
Maracaibo Basin			
Bolívar Coastal	1917	1922	1928
Boscán	1946	1952	1956
Centro	1957	1959	—
CL	1957	1960	—
La Concepción	1924	1950	—
La Paz	1922	1945	1948
Lamar	1958	1959	1963
Las Cruces	1916	1928	1946
Los Claros	1960	1964	—
Mara	1945	1948	1951
Mene Grande	1914	1925	1932
North Lamar	1958	1961	—
Urdaneta	1956	1959	—
Barinas Basin			
Silvestre	1948	1953	—
Sinco	1953	1956	1966
Maturín Basin			
Aguasay	1955	1961	—
Boca	1951	1964	—
Chimire	1948	1952	1955
Dación	1950	1956	1961

Giant Field	Year Discovered	Year Recognised	Year Produced its 100 millionth barrel
East Guara	1940	1945	1948
West Guara	1942	1947	1951
Jusepín	1938	1942	1945
Las Mercedes	1941	1951	1961
Leona	1940	1955	—
Limón	1951	1962	—
Mata	1954	1957	1961
Merey	1954	1963	—
Morichal	1958	1965	—
Nardo	1954	1964	—
Nipa	1945	1950	1955
Oficina	1933	1940	1945
Oritupano	1954	1962	—
Oscurote	1952	1958	—
Oveja	1942	1957	—
Pedernales	1933	1951	—
Quiriquire	1928	1934	1938
San Joaquín	1939	1944	—
Santa Ana	1941	1947	—
Santa Rosa	1941	1948	1959
Soto	1951	1958	1961
Temblador	1936	1950	—
Trico	1941	1957	—
Yopales	1937	1951	—
Zapatos	1955	1962	—

APPENDIX 5. CONCESSIONS AND ASSIGNMENTS

Year	Concessions	Assignments
1951	6,292,761	—
1954	6,026,552	—
1957	6,691,246	—
1960	4,718,445	—
1963	3,558,369	271,968
1966	2,830,178	371,968
1967	2,641,515	671,968

Areas in hectares
As of December 31 of year shown

Source: Ministry of Mines and Hydrocarbons

APPENDIX 6. DATA ON REFINERIES
(Year 1966)

Refinery	Company	Volume processed (barrels)
Amuay	Creole	138,908,623
Cardón	Shell	129,626,985
Puerto La Cruz	Gulf	56,372,182
El Palito	Mobil	29,649,803
Bajo Grande	Chevron	23,299,589
Caripito	Creole	21,312,541
El Chaure	Sinclair	13,486,206
San Lorenzo	Shell	10,989,608
Tucupita	Texas	2,279,417
San Roque	Phillips	1,621,120
Morón	CVP	746,555
San Silvestre	Mobil	167,290
Casigua	Shell	1,667
	Total	428,381,586

Source: Ministry of Mines and Hydrocarbons

APPENDIX 7. PETROLEUM RESOURCES BY BASINS

Basin	Area (km²)	Net volume of sediments (km³)	Resources (bbl x 10⁶)
Maracaibo	55,800	295,000	51,200
Falcón	35,000	275,000	400
Maturín	128,000	333,700	15,100
Barinas	95,000	167,000	2,400
Cariaco	14,000	21,000	100
Gulf of Venezuela	20,000	95,000	Not Estimated
	347,800	1,186,700	69,200

Resources means estimated ultimate volume
of the cumulative production
Net volume refers to sediments above –25,000 feet
and more than 1,000 feet thick
Estimate of the Maturín basin excludes *tar belt*
Source: "Our Gift, Our Oil", Martínez

APPENDIX 8. LARGEST TWENTY FIELDS

	Resources (bbl x 10^6)
1. Bolívar Coastal	16,500
2. Lamar	1,000
3. La Paz	905
4. Quiriquire	810
5. Boscán	675
6. Mene Grande	615
7. Oficina	610
8. Mara	425
9. Urdaneta	350
10. Nipa	340
11. Chimire	315
12. West Guara	260
13. Santa Rosa	240
14. Mata	230
15. Los Claros	220
16. Sinco	215
17. Jusepín	210
18. Centro	200
19. Dación	200
20. East Guara	195

Source: "Giant Fields of Venezuela", Martínez, AAPG

APPENDIX 9. PRODUCTION AND EXPORTS

Year	Production	Exports
1950	546.8	494.2
1955	787.4	747.7
1960	1,041.7	950.4
1961	1,065.8	976.7
1962	1,167.9	1,067.0
1963	1,185.5	1,089.8
1964	1,241.8	1,149.4
1965	1,267.6	1,157.0
1966	1,230.5	1,134.5
1967	1,292.9	1,292.1

Volumes in million barrels

APPENDIX 10. REFINING CAPACITY AND THROUGHPUT

Company	Refinery	Refining capacity		Throughput
		1961	1966	1966
Chevron	Bajo Grande	32,500	57,500	63,800
Creole	Amuay		435,000	380,600
	Caripit }	421,300	74,200	58,400
CVP	Morón	2,300	2,300	2,000
Mobil	El Palito	55,600	80,000	81,200
	San Silvestre	400	500	500
Phillips	San Roque	3,600	4,300	4,500
Shell	Cardón	283,000	315,000	355,200
	San Lorenzo	35,000	35,000	30,100
	Casigua			
	El Calvario }	1,600	1,600	500
	La Rivera			
Sinclair	El Chaure	38,000	38,000	36,700
Texas	Tucupita	10,000	10,000	6,200
Venezuelan-Gulf	Puerto La Cruz	153,300	159,000	154,400
		1,037,300	1,212,400	1,173,600

Volumes in barrels per calendar day
Source: Ministry of Mines and Hydrocarbons, OPEC

APPENDIX 11. PIPELINES

Line	Oil Company	Length (km)	Volume transported 1966 (bbl x 10^6)
BCF/Puerto Miranda	Shell	107	198.2
Ulé/Amuay (x 2)	Creole	230	190.5
Palmarejo de Mara/Cardón	Shell	246	144.0
Anaco/Puerto la Cruz (x 2)	Mene Grande	98	86.4
Oficina/Puerto la Cruz	Mene Grande	156	80.7
Lama/Altagracia	Texaco	95	37.9
Anaco/Puerto la Cruz (x 2)	Mobil	101	34.7
Silvestre/El Palito	Mobil	337	30.8
Travieso/Puerto la Cruz	Mene Grande	153	9.1
Casigua/Lake Maracaibo	Shell	136	4.3
Temblador/Caripito	Creole	150	3.8
Las Mercedes/Puerto la Cruz	Las Mercedes	252	2.3

Gas			(ft^3 x 10^9)
(All lines)	Shell	617	55.4
Santa Rosa/San Joaquín	Mene Grande	19	46.8
(All lines)	CVP	839	43.8
(All lines)	VAT	450	36.9
Roblecito, Placer/Lechozo	VAR	87	17.4
Anaco/Puerto la Cruz	EVGT	107	15.5
Quiriquire/Caripito	Creole	19	4.5

VAT Venezuelan Atlantic Transmission
VAR Venezuelan Atlantic Refining
EVGT Eastern Venezuela Gas Transmission
Source: Ministry of Mines and Hydrocarbons

APPENDIX 12. DESTINATION OF EXPORTS (Year 1966)

		Crude and products (bbl x 10^6)	%
North America		619.5	54.9
of which	US	512.5	45.5
	Canada	105.4	9.3
Europe		227.2	20.1
of which	CEE	76.4	6.8
	UK	84.5	7.5
	Sweden	22.6	2.0
	Spain	20.5	1.8
Central America		127.1	11.2
of which	Puerto Rico	55.2	4.9
	Panama	25.2	2.2
South America		118.6	10.4
of which	Trinidad	55.0	4.9
	Brasil	27.5	2.4
Asia		30.8	2.7
Africa		8.5	0.8
Oceania		2.3	0.2
Others		0.7	0.1
		1,134.5	100.4

Source: Ministry of Mines and Hydrocarbons

APPENDIX 13. INTERNAL CONSUMPTION

	1955	1960	1965	1966
Gasolines	10.27	15.01	18.65	19.81
Kerosene	2.82	3.50	4.01	3.98
Diesel Oil	2.63	4.12	5.56	5.82
Fuel Oil	2.88	2.84	3.01	3.34
Lubricants	0.06	0.21	0.51	0.49
Asphalt	0.84	1.05	2.03	1.88
Turbo Fuel	0.02	0.14	0.28	0.33
Parafine	0.03	0.07	0.14	0.13
Others	0.04	0.09	0.24	0.27
	19.57	27.12	34.43	36.04

Volumes in million barrels
Source: Ministry of Mines and Hydrocarbons

APPENDIX 14. FINANCIAL

	1955	1960	1966
Income	5,875	7,289	10,709
of which crude sales	4,245	4,759	6,755
products sales	1,512	2,347	3,589
Operating costs	1,696	2,403	2,546
Net earnings	1,710	1,282	2,490
Net fixed assets	5,649	9,772	7,039
Working capital	1,091	842	1,177
Capital	6,656	10,406	7,613
Capital expenditures	928	730	633
Paid dividends	1,816	1,357	1,959
Fiscal payments	1,857	2,711	4,880
of which royalties	1,019	1,503	2,531
income tax	712	1,070	2,246

Figures in million bolívars

Source: Ministry of Mines and Hydrocarbons

REFERENCES

This is not a complete listing of all the books, scientific publications, magazines and other documents I have consulted; it only includes the most important sources, arranged by subjects, in chronological order.

GENERAL

A. ROJAS. *Primer libro de geografía de Venezuela según Codazzi.* Caracas: Rojas Hnos., 1870

M. TEJERA. *Venezuela pintoresca e ilustrada.* París: Lib. Española (E. Denné Schmitz), 1875

W. SIEVERS. *Venezuela.* Hamburg: Friederichsen, 1888

C. RICHARDSON. *The Modern asphalt pavement.* London, 1908

L. V. DALTON. *Venezuela.* London: Fisher Unwin, 1912

P. H. GIDDENS. *The birth of the oil industry.* New York: Macmillan, 1938

M. W. BALL. *This fascinating oil business.* Indianapolis: Bobbs-Merril, 1940

B. T. BROOKS. *Peace, plenty and petroleum.* Lancaster (Pa): Jacques Cattett Press, 1944

L. M. FANNING. *Our oil resources.* New York: McGraw-Hill, 1945

H. D. and F. HEDBERG. *Bibliografía e índice de la geología de Venezuela.* Caracas: Lit. del Comercio, 1945

R. A. LIDDLE. *The geology of Venezuela and Trinidad.* Ithaca (NY): Paleont. Research Inst., 1946

M. R. EGAÑA. *Tres décadas de producción petrolera.* Caracas: Tip. Americana, 1947

J. BESSON. *Historia del Estado Zulia.* Maracaibo: Ed. Hnos. Belloso Rosell; T. I, 1943; T. II, 1945; T. III, 1949; T. IV, 1951; T. V, 1957

T. POLANCO MARTINEZ. *Esbozo sobre historia económica venezolana (1498-1810).* Caracas: Ed. Ancora, 1950

ILO (International Labour Office). *Freedom of association and conditions of work in Venezuela.* Geneva, 1951

A. D. AGUERREVERE. *Elementos de derecho minero.* Caracas: Ed. Ragón, 1954

R. W. HIDY and M. E. HIDY. *Pioneering in big business; The resurgent years.* New York: Harper & Bros., 1955 and 1956

E. LIEUWEN. *Petroleum in Venezuela.* Berkeley: U. California Press, 1955

M. M. H. (Ministerio de Minas e Hidrocarburos). *Léxico estratigráfico de Venezuela.* (Also in English.) Caracas: Ed. Sucre, 1956

R. GONZALEZ MIRANDA. *Estudios acerca del régimen legal del petróleo en Venezuela.* Caracas: Fac. Derecho, U. Central, 1958

HNO. N. MARIA. *Los Orígenes de Maracaibo.* Maracaibo: U. del Zulia, 1959

R. ARNOLD, G. MACREADY and TH. BARRINGTON. *The first big oil hunt.* New York: Vantage Press, 1960

W. D. and A. MARSLAND. *Venezuela through its history.* New York: Crowell, 1961

M. M. H. (Ministerio de Minas e Hidrocarburos). *Venezuela and OPEC.* Caracas: Imp. Nacional, 1962

J. P. PEREZ ALFONZO. *Petróleo, jugo de la tierra.* Caracas: Ed. Arte, 1961

J. PRIETO SOTO. *El Chorro: gracia o maldición.* Maracaibo: U. del Zulia, 1962

S. DE LA PLAZA. *Desarrollo económico.* Caracas: U. Central, 1962.

J. A. CLARK. *The chronological history of the petroleum and natural gas industry.* Houston: Clark Book Co., 1963

A. R. MARTINEZ. *Nuestro Petróleo.* Madrid: Ed. Gráficas Minerva, 1963

VOSA (Venezuelan Oil Scouting Association). *Catalogue of Venezuelan Oilfields and Wells, 1878-1961.* (Also Supplements for 1962, 1963, 1964, 1965 and 1966). Caracas, 1963

G. MORON. *History of Venezuela.* London: Allen & Unwin, 1964

C. ROMERO and L. G. ARCAY. *Indice de leyes vigentes.* Caracas: Mene Grande Oil Co., 1964 (and supp. 1965)

C. BALESTRINI. *La industria petrolera en Venezuela.* Caracas: Ministerio de Minas e Hidrocarburos, 1966

BCV (Banco Central de Venezuela). *La economía venezolana en los últimos veinticinco años.* Caracas: BCV, 1966

CREOLE (Creole Petroleum Corp.). *Historia de la industria petrolera en Venezuela.* (F. B. Baptista). Caracas, 1966

CREOLE. *Temas petroleros.* Caracas, 1966

A. R. MARTINEZ. *Our gift, our oil.* Dordrecht (Holland): Reidel, 1966

R. SADER PEREZ. *Petróleo nacional y opinión pública.* Caracas: Ed. Ofidi, 1966

M. EL-SAYED. *L'organization des pays exportateurs de pétrole.* París: Ed. Lib. Gen. Droit et Jurisp., 1967

A. SIVOLI. *Venezuela y sus riquezas mineras.* Caracas: Ed. Cuatricentenario, 1967

EARLY REFERENCES TO VENEZUELAN OIL

GONZALO FERNANDEZ DE OVIEDO Y VALDES. *Historia natural y general de las indias islas y tierra—firme del mar oceano.* Sevilla, 1535 (1st. part); 1540 (2nd. part)

FRANCISCO LOPEZ DE GOMARA. *Historia general de las indias . . .* Zaragoza, 1552

RODRIGO DE ARGÜELLES and GASPAR DE PARRAGA. *Descripcion de la Ciudad de Nueva Zamora, su termino y laguna de Maracaybo.* Archivo Gen. Indias, Indif. Gen., 1579

JUAN DE CASTELLANOS. *Elegías de varones ilustres de indias.* Madrid, 1589

ANTONIO DE HERRERA. *Historia general de los hechos de los castellanos en las islas y tierra firme del mar oceano.* Madrid, la. Década, 1730

P. JOSEPH GUMILLA. *Historia natural, civil y geografica de las naciones situadas en las riveras del rio Orinoco.* Barcelona, 1791

FRANCOIS (RAYMOND JOSEPH) DEPONS. *Voyage a la partie orientale de la Terre-Ferme, dans l'Amérique Méridionale . . .* París, 1806

ALEXANDER VON HUMBOLDT and AIME BONPLAND. *Reise in die Aequinoctial—Gegenden des neuen Continents . . .* Stuttgart u. Tübingen, (1807) 1815

J. J. DAUXION LAVAYSSE. *Voyage aux Iles de Trinidad, de Tabago, de la Marguerite et dans diverses parties de Vénézuéla, dans l'Amérique Méridionale.* París, 1813

A. CODAZZI. *Sumario de la geografia de Venezuela.* París, 1841

TECHNICAL AND OTHER REFERENCES

H. KARSTEN. *Beitrag zur Kenntniss der Gesteine des nordlichen Venezuela.* Zeit. Deutschen Geol. Gesell., vol. 2, pp. 345-361, map. Berlin 1850

H. KARSTEN. *Über die geognostischen Verhaltnisse des nordlichen Venezuela.* (Dr. C. J. B. Karsten) Archiv. f. Min. Geogn., Berg. u. Hutten. Vol. 24, No. 2, pp. 440-470; 1852

H. KARSTEN. *Geognostischen Bemerkungen über die Ungebungen von Maracaybo und über die Nordküste von Neu—Granada.* (Dr. C. J. B. Karsten) Archiv. f. Min. Geogn., Berg, u. Hutten. Vol. 25, No. 2, pp. 567-573; 1853

G. P. WALL. *On the geology of a part of Venezuela and Trinidad.* Geol. Soc. London, Quart. Jour., Vol. 16, pp. 460-70, Map; 1860

W. BRICEÑO MENDEZ. *Informe presentado al Poder Ejecutivo (del Edo. Zulia) sobre la exploración de la región carbonífera de Tulé y los depósitos de petróleo, betunes, asfaltos y carbón que contiene el Estado.* Rep. "El Zulia Ilustrado", Nos. 19, 20, 21, 22 and 23: Ed. facsímil, Fund. Belloso, Maracaibo (1965); 1876

CH. BULLMAN. *Mineral resources of Venezuela.* Eng. Min. Jour. (New York), Vol. 45, pp. 340-342; 1888

W. SIEVERS. *Die Cordillere von Mérida nebst Bemerkungen über das Karibische Gebirge.* (Prof. Penck) Geog. Abhand., Vol. III, No. 1, Wien (Holzel), 1888

E. FORTIN. *Une plaine de bitume au Vénézuéla.* C. R. Soc. Geog. (París), Nos. 11 & 12, pp. 221-224, 1895

H. EGGERS. *Die Asphalt-Quellen am See von Maracaibo.* Deutsche Geogr. Blatt. (Bremen), Vol. 19, No. 41, pp. 103-194, map; 1896

W. SIEVERS. *Ein Schlammvulcan, Hervidero, in den Llanos von Maturín.* (Prof. Umlautt) Deutsche Rundschau, year 20, No. 9. Wien (Hartleben), 1893

E. CORTESE. *Escursioni Geologiche al Venezuela.* Soc. Geol. Italiana, Boll., Vol. XX, No. 3, pp. 447-469; 1901

H. HIRZEL. *Erdöl und asphalt auf den Inseln Pedernales, Pesquero und del Plata in Venezuela.* Chem. Rev. über Fett u. Harz Ind, Vol. 10, No. 12, pp. 275-277; 1903

L. V. DALTON. *On the geology of Venezuela.* Geol. Mag. (London), Vol. 9, No. 575, pp. 203-210; 1912

G. W. HALSE. *Oil Fields of West Buchivacoa, Venezuela.* American Assoc. Pet. Geol., Bull., Vol. 31, No. 8, pp. 1238-1244; 1937

J. H. REGAN. *Notes on the Quiriquire Oil Field, District Piar, State of Monagas.* Bol. Geol. Min. (Venezuela), Vol. 2, No. 2-4, pp. 187-201; 1938

H. D. HEDBERG *et al. Oil Fields of Greater Oficina Area, Central Anzoátegui, Venezuela.* American Assoc. Pet. Geol., Bull., Vol. 31, No. 12, pp. 2089-2169; 1947

H. J. FUNKHOUSER *et al. Santa Ana, San Joaquín and Santa Rosa*

198

Oil Fields, Central Anzoátegui, Venezuela. American Assoc. Pet. Geol., Bull., Vol. 32, No. 10, pp. 1851-1908; 1948

J. E. POGUE. *El petróleo en Venezuela.* Assoc. Venezolana Geol. Min. Pet., Bol., vol. 1, No. 1, pp. 85-145; 1949

G. ZULOAGA. *"Venezuela",* in *World Geography of Petroleum.* American Geog. Soc., Pub. No. 31, pp. 49-79; 1950

E. MONSALVE CASADO. *La lección del petróleo.* Caracas, 1952

J. M. PATTERSON and J. G. WILSON. *Oil Fields of Mercedes Region, Venezuela.* American Assoc. Pet. Geol., Bull., Vol. 37, No. 12, pp. 2705-2733; 1953

(HNO. N. MARIA). *Petróleo de Cubagua para su majestad la Reina.* Rev. "El Farol", CLXXVI, May-June, 1958

J. M. SISO MARTINEZ. *"Ciento cincuenta años de vida republicana",* in *150 años de vida republicana.* Caracas: Ed. Pres. de la República, 1963

D. BENDAHAN. *La contratación colectiva en la industria venezolana del petróleo.* Rev. Col. Abogados Dto. Federal (Venezuela), No. 129, pp. 203-226; 1965

J. TELLO. *Historia del Petróleo en Venezuela.* "El Farol": 218, pp. 6-9; 219, pp. 38-40; 220, pp. 36-41; 1966-67

OTHER REFERENCES:

BVC (Banco Central de Venezuela). *Memoria* (annual); *Memoria Especial 1961-1965*; Actividades Petroleras en . . . (separatas Memoria)

CVP. (Corporación Venezolana del Petróleo). *Annual reports*

MMH. (Ministerio de Minas e Hidrocarburos). *Anuario petrolero y minero de Venezuela* (pub. from 1949 to 1956); *Memoria; Petróleo y otros datos estadísticos* (annual from 1958); *Carta Semanal*

OPEC (Organization of the Petroleum Exporting Countries). *Background information* and other miscellaneous reports. Geneva and Vienna

Skinner's. *Oil & Petroleum year book*

AAPG (American Assoc. Petroleum Geologists). *Foreign exploration developments, "Venezuela";* in explor. issue (July or August)

AVGMP (Asoc. Venezolana Geología, Minería y Petróleo). *Boletín Informativo.* (Monthly)

Boletín de la Riqueza Pública (Est. by R. Andueza Palacio, pub. from 1891 to 1893)

Boletín de la Sociedad Venezolana de Geólogos (from 1965)

El Farol. (House organ of Creole Petroleum Corp.)

El Zulia Ilustrado (1888-1891) Ed. facsímil, Fund. Belloso, Maracaibo, 1965

Ministerio de Fomento. *Revista de Fomento* (Later *Revista de Hidrocarburos y Minas* (1950-1957)

The Oil and Gas Journal (weekly) (in particular "World Wide Oil" issue, last of each year). Tulsa, Okla.

Petróleo Interamericano (Monthly); Tulsa, Okla.

Petroleum Press Service (Monthly); London

Platt's Oilgram News Service (Daily), New York

Venezuelan Economic Review (Weekly) Caracas

Venezuela Up-to-date (Monthly), Embassy of Venezuela, Washington,

VOSA (Venezuela Oil Scouting Assoc.) *Weekly Newsletter*

El Nacional (Caracas daily); *Panorama* (Maracaibo daily)

INDEX

Numbers refer to pages. There might be more than one reference to the item in the indicated page. When a hyphen is used, there is at least one reference in each of the indicated pages.

203

Mingo fd., 157
Misoa, 30; fd., 46
Mito Juan, 149, 156
Mobil, 140, 161
Monagas (State), 28, 41, 42, 92, 122, 140
Monagas, José Gregorio, 27
Monal fd., 98
Monsalve Casado, Ezequiel, 94
Monsanto, Luis Emilio, 94
Montbars, 22
Monte Claro fd., 54
Montevideo, 155, 162
Moquete area, 82
Morales Crespo, 156
Morgan, 22
Morichal fd., 127
Morón ref., 145, 154
Motatán fd., 71, 105
Mud volcano, 28, 36
Mulata area, 76
Muri area, 78
1-MZX fd., 100

Nardo fd., 101, 111
National Development Council, 152;
    Economic C., 158; Energy C., 131,
    152, 154
National Pet. Convention, 100
National reserves, 46, 47, 51, 52, 58, 70, 139
Natural gas, 70, 155, 162
Nau, 22
Navarro, Pedro Vicente, 48
Netick fd., 58
New York & Bermúdez Co., 34, 37, 40,
    42, 43
Nidos fd., 113
Nieblas fd., 112
Nigua fd., 108
Nipa fd., 84
No concessions policy, 91, 137
NOM (Shell) 70, 71, 80
North Cachama fd., 104
North Chimire fd., 106
North Guara fd., 122
North Lamar fd., 126
North Nipa fd., 120
North Oficina fd., 74
North Oscurote fd., 106
North Santa Rosa fd., 125
North Soto fd., 106
North Venezuelan Petroleum, 39, 55
North Yopales fd., 81
North Zumo fd., 118
Nueva Cádiz, 20, 21
Nueva Esparta (State), 42

Oca fd., 110
Oficina-1, 62, 63, 67, 68, 145
Oficina fd., 68, 84, 145
Oficina group of fds., 66, 73, 115

Oficina Técnica de Hidrocarburos *see*
    Technical Off.
Olavarría, Manuel, 28
Oleos fd., 115
Ollas, Las, fd., 75
OPEC, 129, 134, 136–144, 146, 147, 149–
    151, 159, 161–163
Ordenanzas de Minería *see* Mining
    Ordinances
Orinoco Mining, 164
Orinoco Oil, 58
Orinoco region, 23, 34, 37
Oritupano fd., 95
Orocual fd., 62
Otero, Andrés Germán, 153
Otero Silva, Miguel, 136
Oscurote fd., 102
Ostra fd., 81
Oveja fd., 78

Páez fd., 148
Palacio fd., 86
Palinology, 71
Palmarejo de Mara, 101
Palmas, Las, fd., 57
Palmita fd., 123
Pancoastal, 93, 151
Pantepec, 72
Paraguaná, 91, 96, 101
Paria, gulf of, 76, 112
Paria Operations, 133
Párraga, Gaspar de, 22
Pato fd., 117
Paz, La, 39; fd., 51, 53, 106
Pedernales, 25, 34–36, 41; fd., 63
Pelayo fd., 87
Pérez, Néstor Luis, 65–67, 75
Pérez Alfonzo, J. P., 87, 130, 134, 138, 143,
    144
Pérez Guerrero, Manuel, 144, 146, 154, 156
Pérez Jiménez, M., 105, 124
Perijá, 25, 30, 37
Persian Gulf, 133
Petrobrás, 161
Petroleum Industry Exhibition, 72
Petrolia, 30, 32, 41, 58, 63
Philips, Jorge A., 32
Phillips, 86, 92, 98, 102, 117, 127, 161
Pietri, Alejandro, 65
Pilón fd., 68
Piragua fd., 94
Pirital fd., 62
Pitch, 19, 22–24, 27
Placer fd., 91, 102
Planas, Bernabé, 39, 44, 46, 51
Pogue, J. E., 93
Pollution, 65, 66
Posa, 125, 133
Posted prices, 97, 103, 114, 128, 129, 133,
    134, 141, 150

207

For Product Safety Concerns and Information please contact our EU
representative GPSR@taylorandfrancis.com
Taylor & Francis Verlag GmbH, Kaufingerstraße 24, 80331 München, Germany

www.ingramcontent.com/pod-product-compliance
Ingram Content Group UK Ltd.
Pitfield, Milton Keynes, MK11 3LW, UK
UKHW021828240425
457818UK00006B/114